Easy Make & Learn Projects

The Pilgrims, the Mayflower & More

BY DONALD M. SILVER AND
PATRICIA J. WYNNE

D1568015

SCHOLASTIC
PROFESSIONALBOOKS

NEW YORK • TORONTO • LONDON • AUCKLAND • SYDNEY
MEXICO CITY • NEW DELHI • HONG KONG • BUENOS AIRES

for Ole

Thanks for all you taught us.

DMS AND PJW

Front cover and interior design by Kathy Massaro
Cover and interior artwork by Patricia J. Wynne
Cover photographs by Lorenz Photography

ISBN: 0-439-15277-1
Copyright © 2001 by Donald M. Silver and Patricia J. Wynne.
All rights reserved.
Printed in the U.S.A.

❊ Contents ❊

❄ Introduction ❄

What's Inside

Welcome to *Easy Make & Learn Projects: The Pilgrims, the* Mayflower *& More*. The 15 models in this book will introduce your students to the Pilgrims, their voyage to the "New World," and their settlement in Plymouth. The models will also help students compare the Pilgrims' way of life to that of the Wampanoag, the Native Americans they encountered upon arrival. Featured within each chapter are the following sections:

MODEL ILLUSTRATION
This picture shows how the finished model looks. It can be helpful to use as a reference when making the model.

A LOOK BACK IN TIME
Background information on the chapter's topic and concepts is contained here. Use some or all of this information with the Teaching With the Model section, depending on the level of your students.

MAKING THE MODEL
These easy-to-follow instructions include diagrams for assembling the models.

TEACHING WITH THE MODEL
This section provides a step-by-step lesson map with discussion questions for using the models to teach the chapter's main concepts.

PILGRIM DIARY
Students will be invited to make diary entries as though they were Pilgrims sailing on the *Mayflower* or living at Plymouth Plantation. This section provides suggestions for students to write and/or draw.

EXPLORE MORE!
In this section you'll find related activities to extend your students' investigation of the topic.

Helpful Hints for Model-Making

- If possible, enlarge the pattern pages to make the models easier for students to assemble.

- The thickest black lines on the reproducible pages are CUT lines.

- Dotted lines on the reproducible pages are FOLD lines. When folding, be sure to crease well.

- Some models have slits or windows that require cutting. An easy way to cut them is to use the "pinch method": Use your thumb and forefinger to fold the paper near one line and snip an opening. Then insert the scissors into the opening to make the needed cuts.

- Glue sticks can often be substituted for tape. However, some situations—for example, creating flaps—require tape. Thin tape is easier for students to apply to the models than thicker tape.

- If students will be coloring the models and using tape, have them color first so they won't have to color over the tape.

- If a single model will be handled a great deal, consider making it from heavier paper. Simply paste the reproducible page onto construction paper before assembling or photocopy onto heavier paper.

- Some models are more challenging to assemble than others. You can choose to make these models yourself and use them in the classroom as demonstration tools.

To make authentic-looking old paper for the journals, tear open a brown grocery bag (for each student) to make a flat sheet of paper. Crumple the paper into a ball. Mix about two spoonfuls of soil in a bowl of warm water, and immerse each in water. Then spread out the paper to dry on newspaper. Cut into sheets, add a brown construction paper cover, and bind with string.

Exchanging Worlds Trifold Diorama

Children make a trifold diorama that compares the Old World the Pilgrims left to the "New World" they encountered.

❋ A Look Back in Time ❋

The Pilgrims were the first Europeans to settle in what is now New England. They were farmers who came from a rural area near the town of Scrooby, England. When King James I ordered the Pilgrims to attend only the Church of England and live according to its rules and beliefs, the Pilgrims chose to separate from the Church of England and became known as Separatists. In 1608, after suffering persecution for meeting and praying in secret, some Pilgrims fled to Holland. They settled in the city of Leiden, where they were allowed to worship as they wished. However, after a decade in Holland the Pilgrims found that their children were losing touch with their English heritage. So they returned to England, decided to resettle in North America, and found investors to finance their voyage. In 1620 they set off for what they called the "New World," where they could live as they wanted and be free to practice their faith. Later, Governor William Bradford of Massachusetts referred to the Separatist families as Pilgrims, and the name stayed with them.

Making the Model

1 Photocopy pages 7 and 8. Color, if desired. Cut out all ten pieces along the solid black lines. Set the eight small pieces aside.

2 Lay the OLD WORLD piece on a flat surface. Turn the "NEW WORLD" rectangle upside down and tape it onto the bottom of the OLD WORLD piece, as shown.

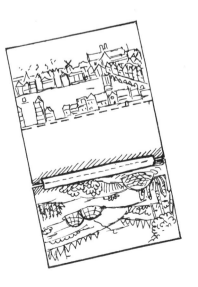

MATERIALS

- reproducible pages 7–8
- scissors
- tape
- crayons, colored pencils, or markers (optional)

3 Fold the taped piece along its dotted lines and tape at the top to make a tentlike shape.

4 Invite students to tape the small pieces to suitable spots on the appropriate sides of their dioramas.

Pilgrim Diary

Tell students to imagine that they are Pilgrims. Ask them to focus on the decision to leave the Old World to sail to North America. Students can make "Why Go?" and "Why Stay?" lists and/or draw pictures of their old and new lives.

A Changing World

Find a map that represents the world at the time of the Pilgrim era. Textbooks are good sources. Have students compare it to a current world map. Are they surprised at how little was known of the land that is now North America? How well informed and prepared for their new home do students think the Pilgrims were?

Teaching With the Model

1 Point out to students that the Old World side of the diorama shows the city of Leiden, in Holland. (See the Moving *Mayflower* Map model on page 14 to help students locate Holland.) The "New World" side shows where the Pilgrims landed in what is now called Massachusetts. Explain to students that although the Pilgrims referred to North America as the "New World," Native American people had already been living there for thousands of years. Then ask:

🦃 Why did the Pilgrims leave England for Holland? (*to escape religious persecution*)

🦃 Why did the Pilgrims eventually choose to leave Holland? (*to return to a more English lifestyle*)

🦃 Why did the Pilgrims decide to go to America? (*so they could live and worship as they wished*)

2 Challenge students to compare the Old World the Pilgrims left to the "New World" they encountered. Have them read the text on each side of the diorama and think about where they chose to place the small pieces. Stimulate student thought and discussion with these questions:

🦃 What did Leiden have that the "New World" didn't? (*city buildings, roads, markets, windmills, and so on*)

🦃 What awaited the Pilgrims in the "New World?" (*wild animals, forests, trails, Native American villages*)

🦃 Where would you have preferred to live? Why?

Old World

In the Old World, where the pilgrims lived, there were cities, towns, houses, roads, and shops.

Exchanging Worlds Trifold Diorama

"New World"

In the "New World" there were Native American villages, trails, wild animals, and forests.

Moving Mayflower Map

*Students trace on a movable map the ship's route
from England to North America*

❄ A Look Back in Time ❄

On September 6, 1620, 51 Pilgrim men, women, and children sailed from Plymouth, England, aboard the *Mayflower*. The King had given the Pilgrims permission to settle in the region around the Hudson River in what is now New York. But stormy weather, rough seas, and heavy rains damaged the ship en route and forced it to turn north to escape treacherous waters. After 66 days at sea, the ship sailed into what is now known as Cape Cod Bay on November 11, 1620. An exploring party then landed where Provincetown, Massachusetts, stands today.

Making the Model

1 Photocopy page 14. Color, if desired. Then cut out the two pieces along the solid black outer lines.

2 Cut a slit along the solid black line on the map side.

3 Fold the VOYAGE OF THE *MAYFLOWER* piece along the dotted midline, and tape together on the sides.

MATERIALS

❧ reproducible page 14
❧ scissors
❧ tape
❧ crayons, colored pencils, or markers (optional)

4 Fold the small ship piece in half along the dotted midline. Fold the ship flaps up and tape as shown.

5 Fold the BASE underneath the flaps and tape as shown.

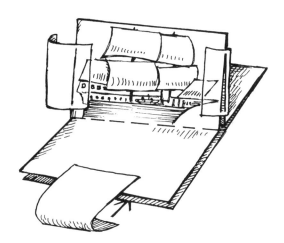

6 Slide the flaps of the ship in between both sides of the slit on the VOYAGE OF THE *MAYFLOWER* piece, facing left, as shown. Make sure the ship can move freely.

Teaching With the Model

After students read the text on the back of their map models, invite them to make the *Mayflower* "sail" from England to Cape Cod. Then ask:

- How long was the voyage? (*66 days*)
- Where did they sail from? (*England*) Where did they land? (*Cape Cod*) Invite students to find these places on their maps.
- What does the compass rose show? (*direction*) In which direction did the Mayflower sail? (*from east to west*)
- Challenge students to explain why Holland is included on the map. (*The Pilgrims lived there for a time before returning to England to sail to America.*)

Peek-Inside Mayflower

Children make a model of the Mayflower and explore the inside of this historic ship.

❄ A Look Back in Time ❄

Nobody knows exactly what the *Mayflower* looked like. The peek-inside model is based on a replica of the ship, built in 1957. It is known that life aboard the *Mayflower* was difficult. The 102 passengers were crammed into a small below-deck space with a ceiling so low that the adults could not stand upright. The air was cold and damp, and rain seeped into cracks. Meals aboard ship consisted mainly of salty dried fish and beef, moldy cheese, and hard, stale biscuits that were infested with bugs. Rough seas made many seasick, and there were no bathrooms. In spite of these harsh conditions, only one man died at sea.

Making the Model

1 Photocopy pages 15 and 16. (Enlarge first, if possible.) Color if desired. Cut out all four pieces along the solid black lines.

2 Place the two larger pieces faceup and tape together, as shown.

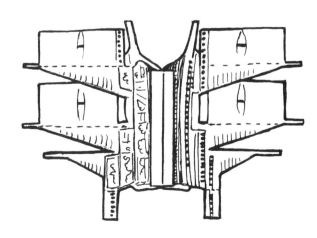

MATERIALS

- reproducible pages 15–16
- scissors
- tape
- glue stick (optional)
- sheet of 9- by 12-inch blue construction paper
- crayons, colored pencils, or markers (optional)

Pilgrim Diary

Tell students to imagine that they are Pilgrims. Challenge them to describe what life is like aboard the *Mayflower*. Encourage them to draw pictures of the ship, the crew, the passengers, and their quarters. What do they eat? What do they do to keep busy?

3 Turn the taped piece facedown. Fold in and overlap the sail pieces along the dotted lines. Tape or glue together. Fold in and overlap the two bow pieces. Tape or glue together. Finally, tape or glue together the two parts of the mast.

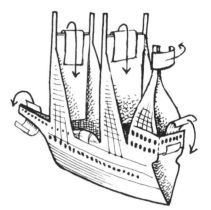

4 Position the model so that the interior of the ship faces you. Tape the third piece facedown to this side of the ship.

5 Fold the FLAG piece in half along the dotted line. Tape or glue the flag onto the mast.

6 To make the waves, fold a sheet of blue construction paper into thirds, widthwise. Tape or glue together the two outside flaps at each end. (This will make a prism shape.) Crease as shown in diagram 6, below. Cut wavy scallops across the top (open edges) of the folded paper. Set the ship in between the waves.

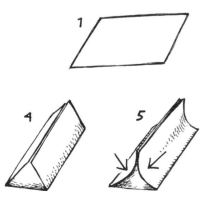

Teaching With the Model

As students look at their models, ask:

🖐 What was life was like aboard the *Mayflower*? (*crowded, cold, lots of seasick people, and so on*)

🖐 Why were the Pilgrims willing to put up with the hardships aboard the *Mayflower*? (*to reach North America, where they could practice their religion and live as they wished*)

🖐 Point out the different sections of the ship, using the diagram and key below.

Explore More!

How Many Days?

The Pilgrims set sail on September 6, 1620, and landed on November 11, 1620. Have students calculate how many days the Pilgrims spent aboard the *Mayflower* by counting days on a calendar. (*66 days, not counting November 11*)

KEY

(A) **ROUND HOUSE** where charts were held and the ship's course plotted

(B) **GREAT CABIN** where the ship's captain slept

(C) **STEERAGE** where a tiller and compass were used to steer the ship

(D) **'TWEEN DECKS** where passengers, including the Pilgrims, stayed

(E) **FO'C'SLE (FOLK-sill)** where the crew's meals were cooked

(F) **HOLD** the place where food, drinks, and supplies were stored

(G) **GUN ROOM** where guns and ammunition were stored

(H) **CAPSTAN** a machine used to lift heavy cargo

(I) **WINDLASS** a machine used to lift the ship's anchor

(J) **BALLAST** rocks that helped keep the ship stable

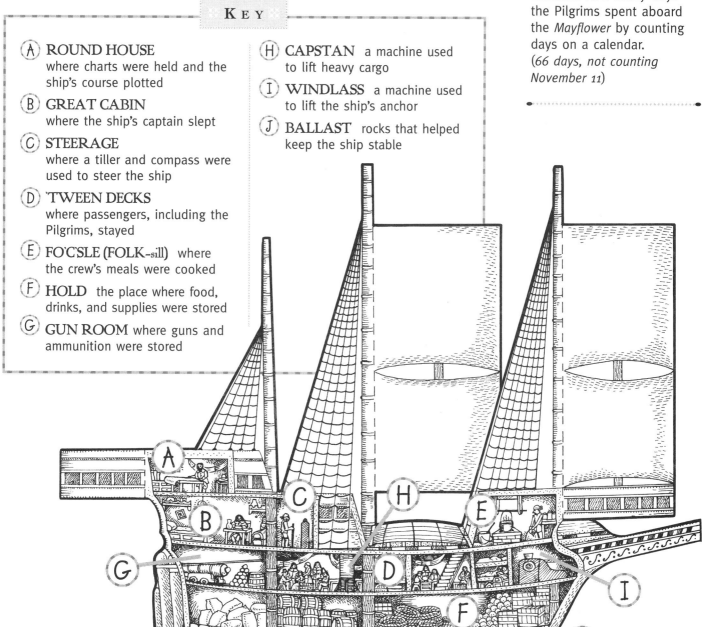

Voyage of the Mayflower

The Pilgrims sailed to North America aboard the Mayflower. While on the ship they agreed to govern themselves and make their own laws when they landed.

✻ ✻ ✻

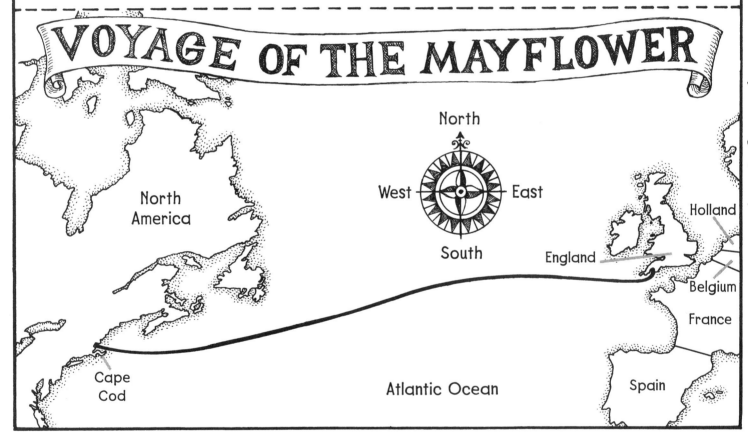

VOYAGE OF THE MAYFLOWER

North

West — East

South

North America

Holland

England

Belgium

France

Cape Cod

Atlantic Ocean

Spain

base

flap

flap

Moving Mayflower
✻ Map ✻

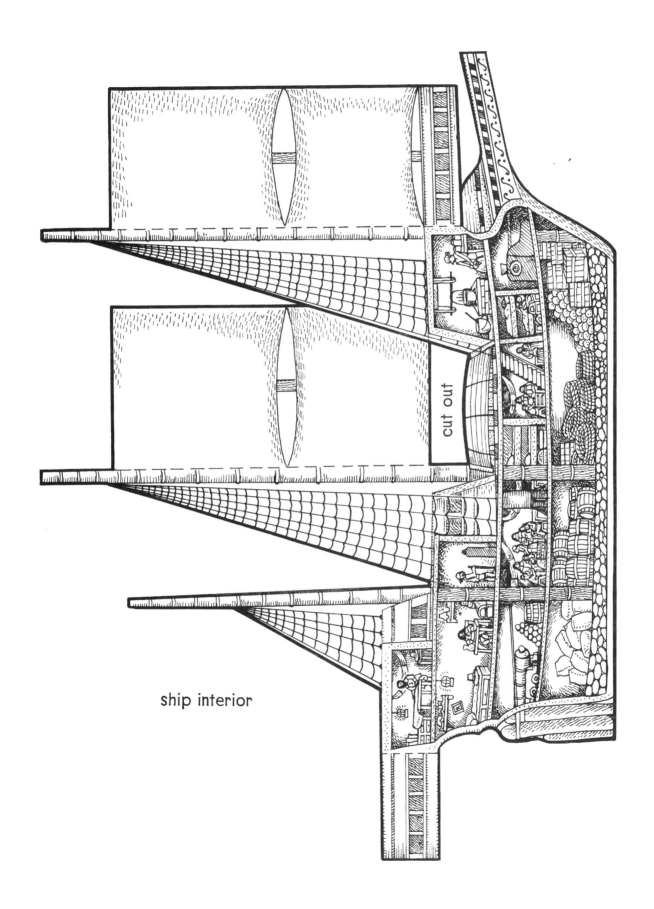

cut out

ship interior

⁂ Peek-Inside Mayflower ⁂

Easy Make & Learn Projects: The Pilgrims, the Mayflower & More Scholastic Professional Books

flag

cut out

ship exterior

ship exterior

Pilgrim Town ❋ Wampanoag Village

Children make and compare models of the first Pilgrim town at Plymouth and of a seventeenth-century Wampanoag village.

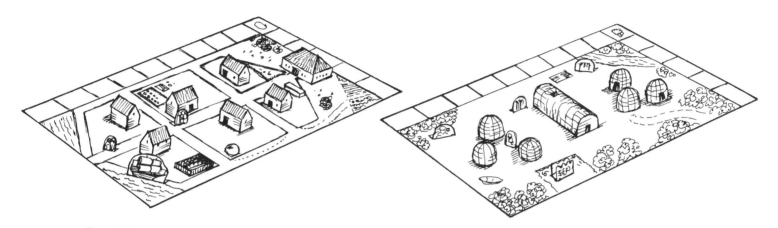

❋ A Look Back in Time ❋

Soon after landing, a Pilgrim exploring party found a hill overlooking a sheltered harbor across Cape Cod Bay. It had a stream and the land had been cleared by past Native American inhabitants. Here the Pilgrims disembarked on December 26, 1620, and founded New Plimoth (now called Plymouth). During this first winter the Pilgrims stayed aboard the *Mayflower* at night and built their village by day. They cut down trees to make boards for wooden buildings and made thatched roofs of reeds and other coarse grasses. The Pilgrims used oiled paper for windowpanes.

They also built a 20- by 20-foot meetinghouse in which to meet and pray. Six cannons were kept there in case of attack. Down from the meetinghouse two rows of houses were built (their sizes are unknown); the inner walls were made of clay. The entire village was surrounded by a tall fence, or palisade.

In February 1620 the Pilgrims sighted Wampanoag (WAHM-puh-NOH-ahg) natives who lived in small nearby villages. The Wampanoag had lived in New England for thousands of years before the arrival of the Pilgrims. In winter the Wampanoag (meaning "People of the Dawn") occupied inland villages with small, round, single-family houses, called wetus (WEE-to's). Each wetu had a frame of long bent and tied poles. The frame was covered with bark and/or woven mats. Mats were also hung in the doorways to keep out wind. Wetus ranged in size between about 10 to 15 feet in diameter. As many as ten people lived inside. Sometimes a larger winter house for several related families, called a neesquttow (nees-KWAH-toh), was also built. In spring the entire village moved to the coast and built a village of wetus.

Making the Models

❊ Pilgrim Town ❊

1 To make this model, consider dividing the class into groups of three or four and letting each group make one Pilgrim town. Have each student in a group make one or two Pilgrim buildings and one other item for the village.

2 Reproduce pages 24–27. (Enlarge them, if possible.) Color, if desired.

3 Cut pages 24 and 25 along the solid black lines. Tape or glue the edge of page 25 to the edge of page 24 where indicated.

4 Cut out the seven Pilgrim buildings on pages 26 and 27 along the solid black lines, and assemble as follows:

❊ Meetinghouse

Fold the MEETINGHOUSE piece along the dotted lines and crease well. First, tape the walls together. Then, tape the roof together, as shown.

❊ Houses

Fold each of the four HOUSE pieces along the dotted lines and crease well. First, tape the walls together. Then, tape the roof of each of the houses.

❊ See-Inside Houses

Fold each of the two HOUSE pieces along the dotted lines and crease well. Note that the walls and roof fold in the same way as the meetinghouse and houses above, but the inside scene strips fold with the printed sides facing each other. First, tape the back wall to each of the house sides. Then, fit the strip inside the house and tape as shown.

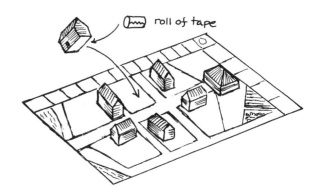

5 Have students use glue or rolled pieces of tape to secure the buildings onto the town grid. The meetinghouse goes into its labeled place on the town grid, and the other six houses each go on one of the six outlined plots.

6 Cut out the remaining seven small pieces along the solid black lines, and assemble as follows:

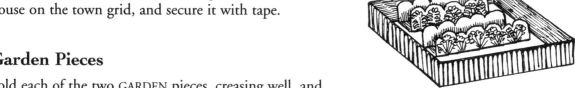

❋ Garden Fence

Fold and tape the GARDEN FENCE together. Set it near a house on the town grid, and secure it with tape.

❋ Garden Pieces

Fold each of the two GARDEN pieces, creasing well, and glue or tape them inside the fence, as shown.

❋ Table

Fold the TABLE along the dotted lines and tape together as shown. Glue or tape it near the meetinghouse on the town grid.

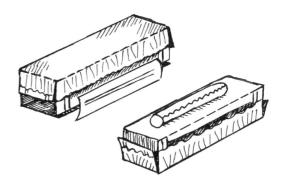

❋ *Mayflower*

Fold the *MAYFLOWER* along the dotted line, and tape or glue it onto the water near the bottom of the town grid.

❋ Pilgrims

Fold the two PILGRIM pieces (PILGRIM FAMILY and HUNTERS) along the dotted lines and tape or glue them onto an appropriate place on the town grid.

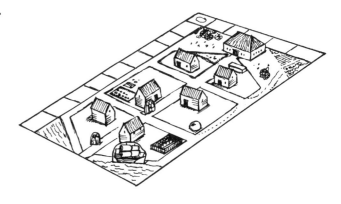

MATERIALS

- reproducible pages 28–31
- scissors
- tape
- glue (optional)
- crayons, colored pencils, or markers (optional)

Wampanoag Village

1 To make this model, consider dividing the class into groups of three or four and letting each group make one Wampanoag village. Have each student in a group make one or two dwellings and one other item for the village.

2 Reproduce pages 28–31. (Enlarge them, if possible.) Color, if desired.

3 Cut pages 28 and 29 along the solid black lines. Tape or glue the edge of page 29 to the edge of page 28 where indicated.

4 Cut out the seven Wampanoag dwellings on pages 30 and 31 along the solid black lines, and assemble as follows:

Neesquttow

Fold the NEESQUTTOW piece along the dotted lines and crease well. Bend the long section over the base and tape as shown. Tape the top to the side walls.

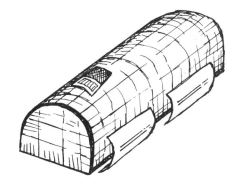

Wetus

- Fold each of the five WETU pieces along the single dotted lines and crease well.

- Wrap the wall section of each WETU piece into a cylinder and tape as shown.

- Secure the circle base to the walls in several places, using small pieces of tape.

- Bend a few of the roof fringes together and tape as shown. Repeat to finish each wetu roof.

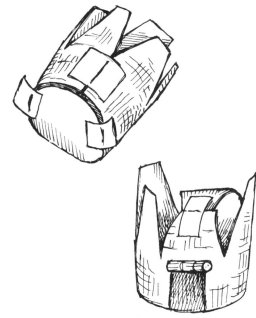

See-Inside Wetu

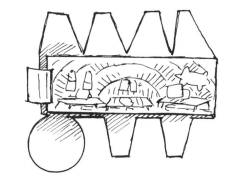

- Fold the SEE-INSIDE WETU piece along the dotted lines and crease well.

- Fold the inside strip back onto the rest of the piece and tape as shown.

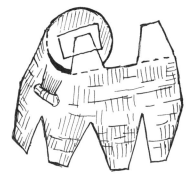

- Bend the wall around the circle base and tape TAB A onto the top of the base. Do the same for TAB B, as shown.

- Bend a few of the roof fringes together and tape as shown.

5 Invite students to place the Wampanoag houses in appropriate spots on the village grid and tape or glue them into place.

6 Cut out the remaining eight small pieces from pages 30 and 31 along the solid black lines.

Canoe

Fold the CANOE piece along the dotted lines and tape as shown. Push the flap down into the bottom of the canoe to hold the sides of the canoe apart. Attach it to the village grid in section I-4.

Smoking Fish

Fold the SMOKING FISH piece along the dotted line and attach it near the fish-smoking racks.

❋ Clamshell Pile

Fold the CLAMSHELL PILE piece along the dotted line and tape or glue onto the waste pile in section I-2.

❋ Corn

Fold the CORN piece along the dotted lines. Tape or glue onto the garden.

❋ Wampanoag

Fold the four WAMPANOAG pieces (WAMPANOAG WOMAN COOKING, WAMPANOAG BRAVES WITH FIVE DEER, WAMPANOAG FAMILY, and WAMPANOAG FISHERMAN) along the dotted lines and tape or glue each onto the village grid, where appropriate.

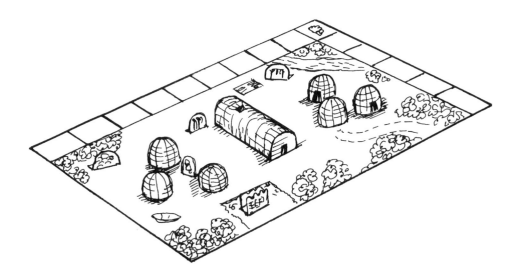

Teaching With the Models

1 Explain to students that both villages are on grid maps. Check students' understanding of the grid maps by asking questions such as:

- In the Pilgrim town, where is the meetinghouse? (*between A-2 and A-4*) What is in section F-1? (*a garden*)
- In the Wampanoag village, where is the waste pile? (*I-2*) What's between C-1 and D-1? (*fish-smoking racks*), and so on.

2 Challenge students to compare the two villages. Ask:

- How are they alike? (*both have houses, gardens, people, and so on*)
- How are they different? (*kinds of houses; position of houses; Pilgrim town is near the ocean, and the Wampanoag village is in the woods.*)

3 The Wampanoag lived in different places during the summer and winter. Ask students if they think this is a spring-summer village or a fall-winter one. Why? (*fall-winter; it's inland and has a neesquttow house*)

Pilgrim Diary

Have students imagine that they are Pilgrims. Invite them to draw a picture of the Pilgrim house they live in at Plymouth, using the model as a guide. Challenge them to describe how it was built and what is inside.

Explore More!

Thatch a Roof

Bring in some dried reeds or other grasses, or use paper raffia. Invite students to make small bundles and tie them together as if for roof thatching. Students can tape a small bundle to the pictures of the homes they drew in their diary.

Measure a Wetu

Let students experience the size of a wetu with this activity. Take the class outside to the school yard (or to the gym), and with the aid of a yardstick, measure out and then cut about seven feet (half the diameter of an average wetu) from a ball of string or yarn. Tie a piece of chalk to one end of the string. Tack the string into the ground or ask a student to stand on the other end while you pull the string taut and draw a circle with the chalk. Let groups of 10 children take turns standing inside the circle. Tell children that this is about the number of people who lived in a wetu of this size.

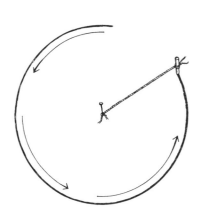

Pilgrim Town ✳

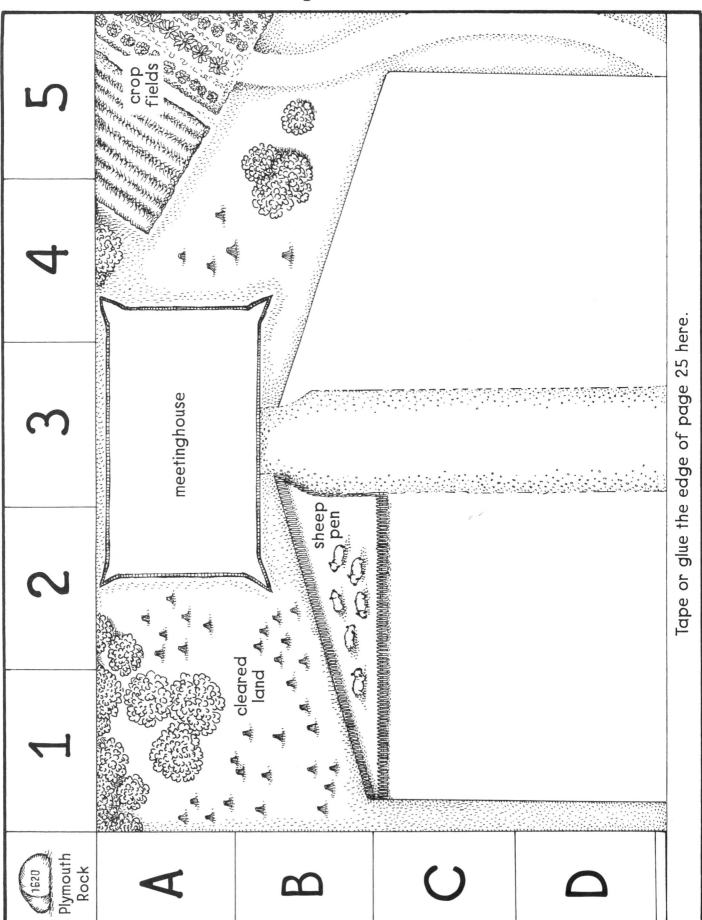

5

4

3

2

1

A

B

C

D

Plymouth Rock
1620

crop fields

meetinghouse

cleared land

sheep pen

Tape or glue the edge of page 25 here.

Easy Make & Learn Projects: The Pilgrims, the Mayflower & More   Scholastic Professional Books

❄ Pilgrim Town ❄

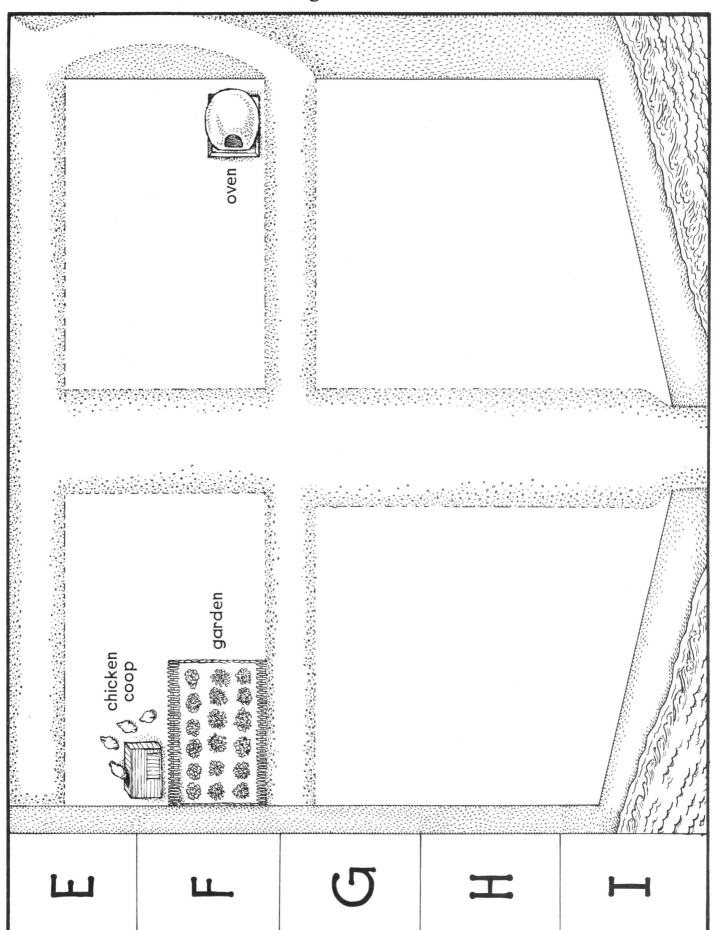

oven

chicken
coop

garden

E

F

G

H

I

Easy Make & Learn Projects: The Pilgrims, the Mayflower & More   Scholastic Professional Books

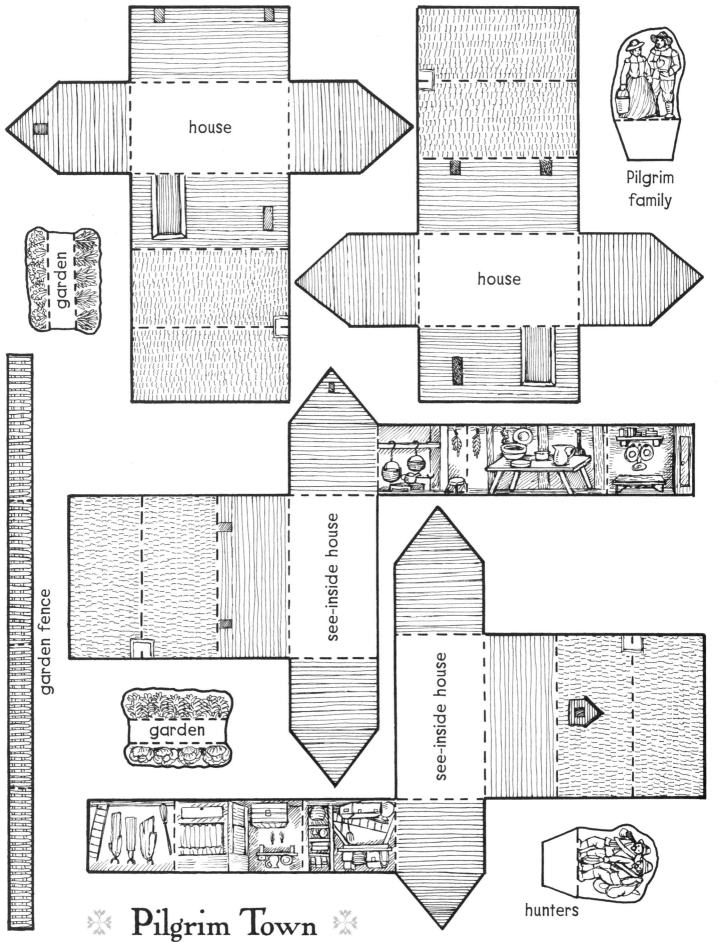

house

house

Pilgrim
family

garden

garden fence

see-inside house

garden

see-inside house

hunters

※ Pilgrim Town ※

Easy Make & Learn Projects: The Pilgrims, the Mayflower & More   Scholastic Professional Books

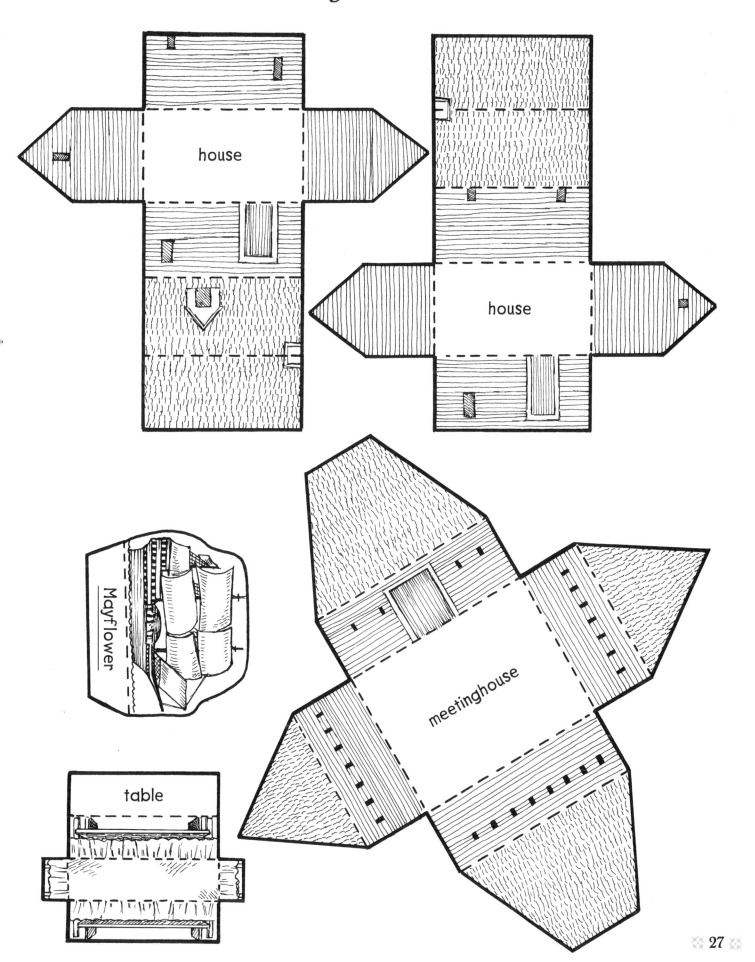

house

house

Mayflower

meetinghouse

table

woods

woods

footpath into the woods

river

woodlands

	1	2	3	4	5
A					
B					
C					
D					

fish-smoking racks

Tape or glue the edge of page 29 here.

Easy Make & Learn Projects: The Pilgrims, the Mayflower & More   Scholastic Professional Books

garden

waste
pile

Easy Make & Learn Projects: The Pilgrims, the Mayflower & More   Scholastic Professional Books

E

F

G

H

I

Wampanoag Village

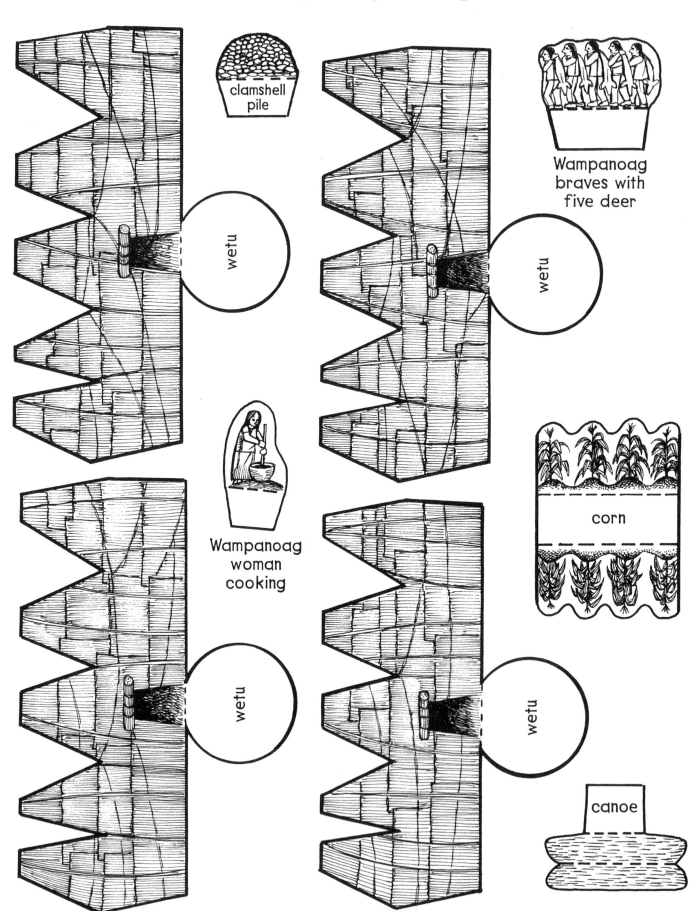

clamshell pile

Wampanoag braves with five deer

wetu

wetu

Wampanoag woman cooking

corn

wetu

wetu

canoe

Wampanoag Village

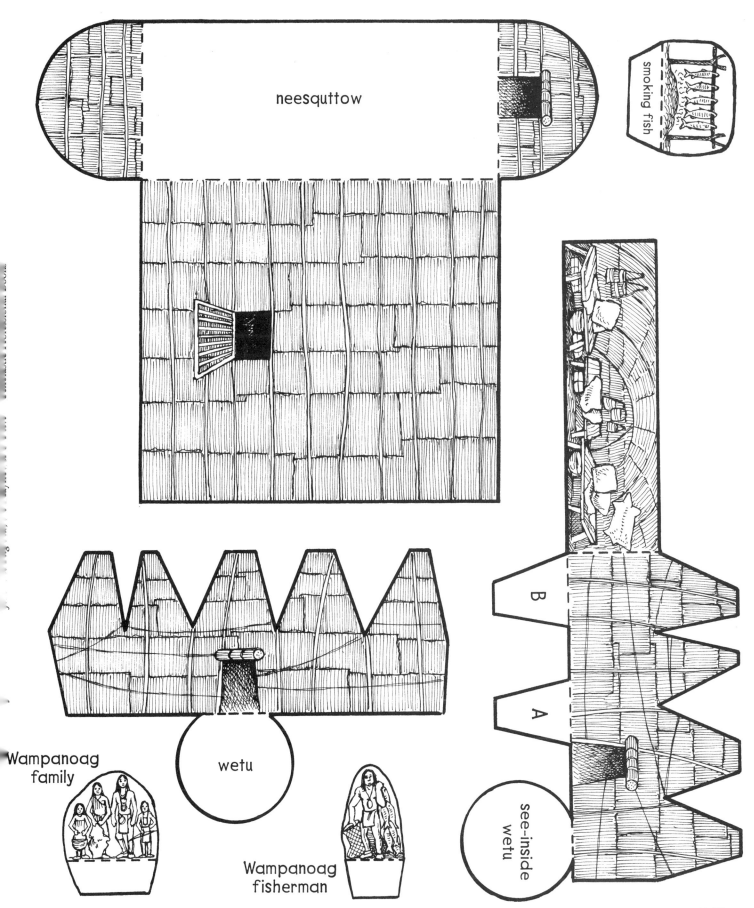

neesquttow

smoking fish

B

A

wetu

Wampanoag family

Wampanoag fisherman

see-inside wetu

Pilgrim Vegetable Patch
❋ ❋ ❋
Wampanoag Garden

*While making these models, children learn about the gardens
planted by the Pilgrims and the Wampanoag of long ago.*

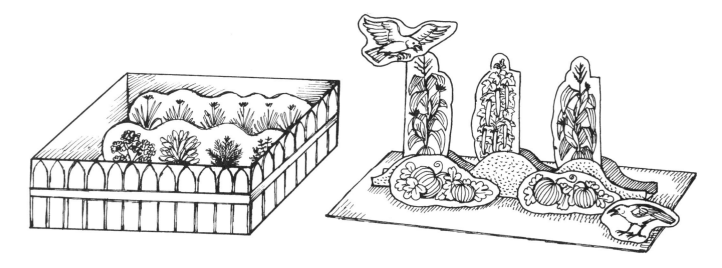

❋ A Look Back in Time ❋

The Pilgrims were farmers, and they brought their skills and seeds with them to the "New World." But the Pilgrims knew nothing about the soil or climate where they settled. They planted their herb and vegetable gardens next to their houses and out in the fields. Some of the seeds they brought with them from England grew, but most did not. Without the help and crops given to them by the Wampanoag, the Pilgrims would not have had enough food to get them through the long winter.

A Wampanoag brave named Squanto taught the Pilgrims about the Wampanoag ways of planting. (Squanto had been kidnapped by explorers, sold into slavery, and then escaped to England, where he learned to speak English.) When planting corn, the Wampanoag made little hills of soil, planted four or five kernels in each hill, and then added a small fish as fertilizer. Squanto taught the Pilgrims when and how to plant beans so that the vines would climb the already grown cornstalks. He also showed them how to plant squash and pumpkins between the mounds and pointed out which local plants were edible.

Making the Models

Pilgrim Vegetable Patch

MATERIALS

- reproducible page 36
- scissors
- tape
- crayons, colored pencils, or markers (optional)
- sheet of green construction paper (optional)

1 Photocopy page 36. (Enlarge, if possible.) Color, if desired. Cut out all six pieces along the solid black lines, and then assemble as follows:

Herbs and Onions

Fold the flaps on the HERBS AND ONIONS pieces along the dotted lines so that they stand up. Set them where indicated on the rectangular piece, and tape into place as shown.

Cabbages

Tape the CABBAGES piece in place as well.

Fence

Fold both FENCE pieces along the dotted lines. Tape them together to make a rectangle, as shown. Then, place the fence around the garden plot. Tape the entire garden onto a sheet of green construction paper, if desired.

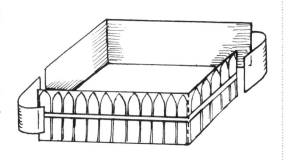

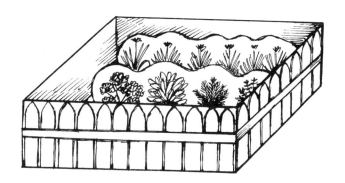

MATERIALS

- reproducible page 37
- scissors
- tape
- crayons, colored pencils, or markers (optional)
- green construction paper (optional)

Wampanoag Garden

1 Photocopy page 37. (Enlarge, if possible.) Color, if desired. Then cut out all 13 pieces along the solid black lines, and assemble as follows:

✤ Garden Mound

Fold up the sides of the GARDEN MOUND piece along the dotted lines. Loosely tape the mounds together where indicated. (OPTIONAL: Tape the garden mound onto construction paper.)

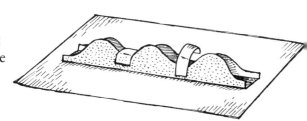

✤ Fish and Seeds

Fold the FISH AND SEEDS pieces along the dotted lines, and drop one into each of the three mounds.

✤ Corn and Beans

Fold the CORN AND BEANS pieces along the dotted lines. Tape one inside each mound, as shown.

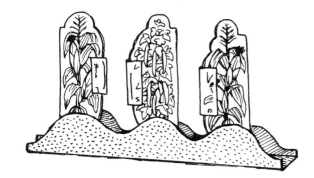

✤ Squash

Tape the SQUASH pieces onto the foot of the mounds (both sides), as shown. Tape the CROWS onto the model, where desired.

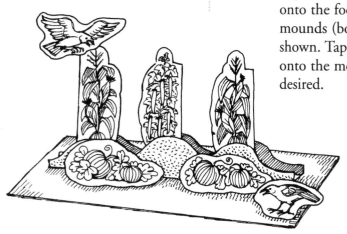

Teaching With the Models

1 After students have assembled the Pilgrim model, ask:

🐦 What crops grew in the Pilgrim garden? (*herbs, cabbages, onions*)

🐦 Where did the Pilgrims get seeds for these plants? (*brought them over from England*)

🐦 Why did they need a fence? (*to keep out chickens, rabbits, and other animals*)

2 After students have assembled the Wampanoag model, ask:

🐦 Why did the Wampanoag of long ago plant a fish with the seeds? (*the fish was used as fertilizer*)

🐦 What plants did the Wampanoag grow? (*corn, squash, beans*)

3 Challenge students to compare the two gardens. How are they different? (*different plants; the Wampanoag of long ago grew plants together whereas the Pilgrims grew plants in separate rows*)

4 Invite students to revisit the Pilgrim town and Wampanoag village (see page 17) and take note of the gardens in each.

Pilgrim Diary

Ask students to write an entry about Squanto's first visit to the village. As Pilgrims, how do they feel when they see this Wampanoag brave approach? Are they surprised that he speaks English? What does he teach them? Students can draw a picture of what they think he looks like. (Students can use the Who Wore What? Wardrobes models on page 54 as a reference.)

Sprout Seeds

Bring in seeds of the plants featured in the models, and allow students to compare them. Students can sprout the seeds in self-sealing plastic bags, lined with moist paper towels, and compare their growth.

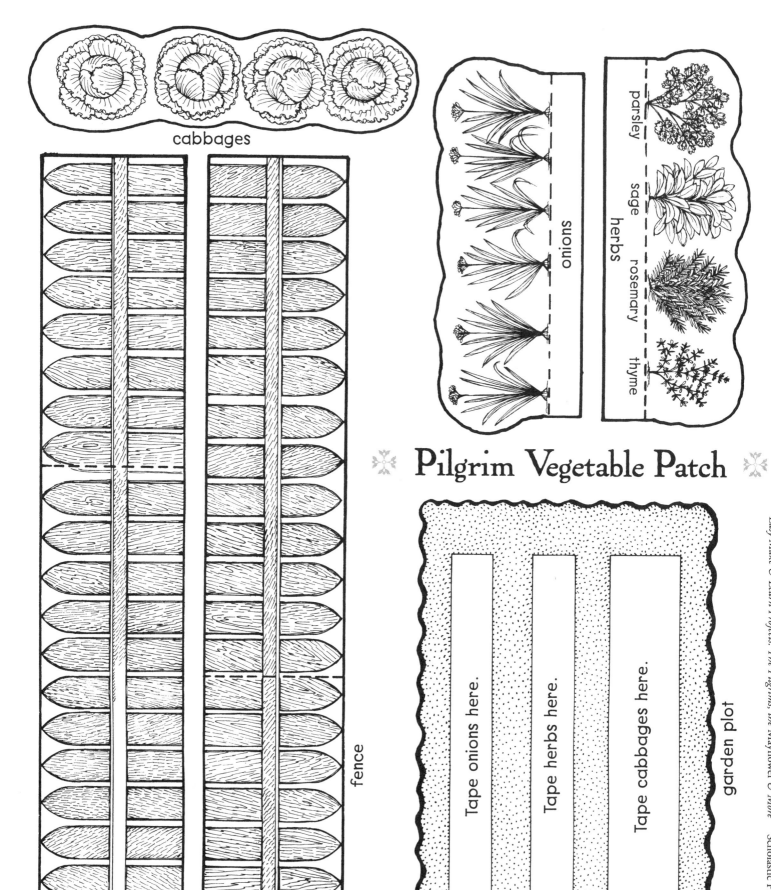

cabbages

parsley

sage

rosemary

thyme

herbs

onions

Pilgrim Vegetable Patch

fence

Tape onions here.

Tape herbs here.

Tape cabbages here.

garden plot

Easy Make & Learn Projects: The Pilgrims, the Mayflower & More   Scholastic Professional Books

Wampanoag Garden

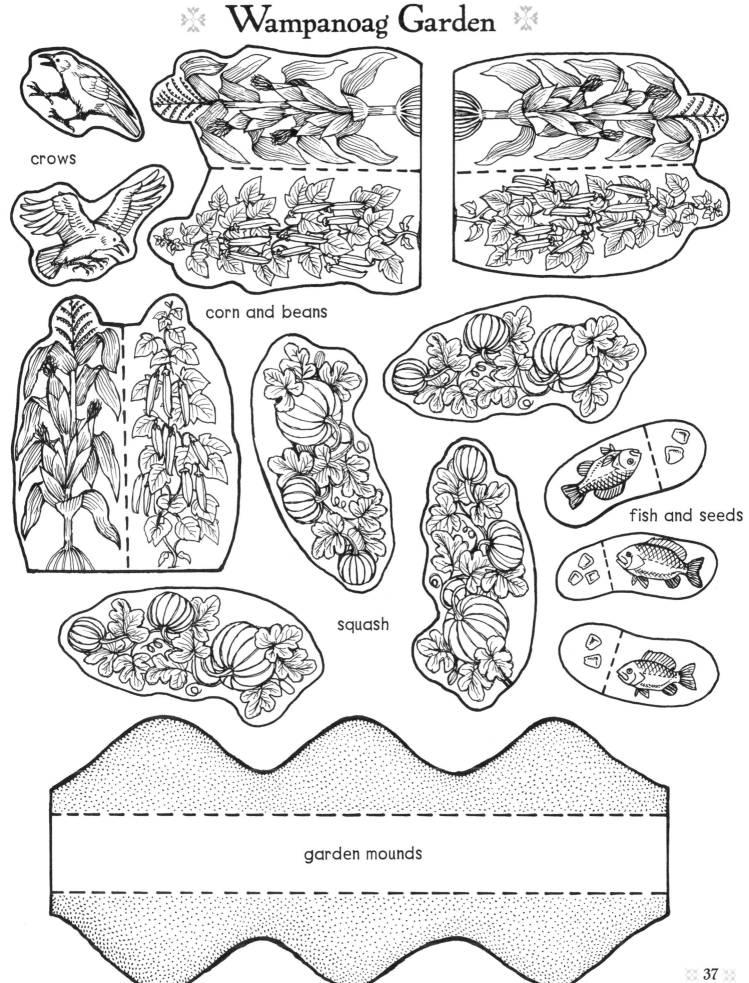

crows

corn and beans

fish and seeds

squash

garden mounds

Easy Make & Learn Projects: The Pilgrims, the Mayflower & More   Scholastic Professional Books

Hunt for Food Match-Up

❋ ❋ ❋

Trap a Fish

Children make models that teach them how the Pilgrims
and the Wampanoag of long ago found food.

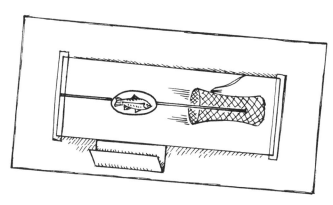

❋ A Look Back in Time ❋

The Pilgrims brought guns and cannons to protect themselves from hostile natives, explorers from other nations, and wild animals. But these farmers knew little about hunting and had few skills as woodsmen. The Wampanoag of long ago, on the other hand, were skilled, silent trackers and expert hunters of deer, raccoons, squirrels, rabbits, turkeys, geese, ducks, and other animals. They fashioned bows, arrows, and spears from wood, and chipped stones to make sharp arrowheads, spearheads, and hatchets. With Squanto's help, the Pilgrims learned to hunt. In exchange, the Wampanoag learned about muskets and traded for metal knife blades.

The Pilgrims also learned fishing skills from the Wampanoag. Unlike the Europeans, who built boats with sails, the Wampanoag made dugout canoes, called mishoons (mih-SHOONS), for fishing and traveling. Using spears, nets, and hooks and lines, the Wampanoag fished for cod and other fishes. They pulled eels from the mud and trapped lobsters. The task of cleaning, cooking, salting, and drying the meat or catch was done by the women and girls. When the tide was low, Pilgrim and Wampanoag women also gathered mussels, clams, and other shellfish along the shore.

Making the Models

Hunt for Food Match-Up

1 Photocopy page 42. Color, if desired. Cut out the seven pieces along the solid black lines.

2 Bring together the two ends of the forest scene to form a cylinder, and tape as shown.

3 Fold out the flaps on the cylinder so that it stands.

4 Tape the CLOUD and the BUSH onto the model as indicated. Make sure to tape only along the bottom of each piece.

5 Hide the GOOSE behind the cloud and the DEER behind the bush.

6 Tape the CLAM-DIGGER piece in place, as indicated. Insert the clams inside the flap, near the bottom.

7 Center the forest scene cylinder on the cardboard and tape or glue in place.

MATERIALS

- reproducible page 42
- scissors
- tape
- crayons, colored pencils, or markers (optional)
- 9- by 10-inch piece of cardboard

MATERIALS

- reproducible page 43
- stapler
- scissors
- tape
- 5- by 11-inch sheet of paper
- crayons, colored pencils, or markers (optional)

Trap a Fish

1 Photocopy page 43. Color, if desired. Cut out the three pieces along the solid black outer lines.

2 Staple the fish to the SLIDER piece, as indicated.

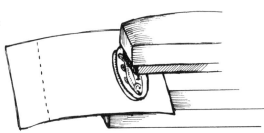

3 Place the long NET piece on a sheet of paper horizontally, as shown. Tape the right side of the piece onto the paper.

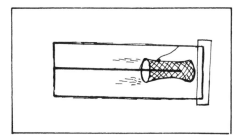

4 Cut out the long solid black line on the rectangle piece so that no black shows.

5 Slip the SLIDER under the rectangle piece, and position the fish on top of the two flaps, as shown.

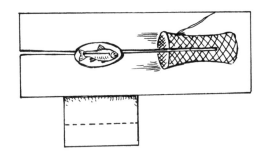

6 Tape the left side of the rectangle piece onto the paper.

7 Fold the SLIDER along the dotted line to make a handle, and slide the fish into the net.

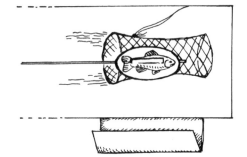

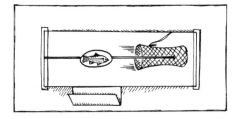

Teaching With the Models

1 Ask students these questions as they study the HUNT FOR FOOD MATCH-UP model:

🦃 Did the Pilgrims bring guns with them to North America? (*yes*) Why? (*protection*)

🦃 Why weren't the Pilgrims good hunters? (*They were farmers with little hunting experience.*)

🦃 Why were the Wampanoag better hunters than the Pilgrims? (*They had more practice, hunted for survival, were familiar with the woods, could identify animal tracks, and their bows and shoes made less noise than the Pilgrims' guns and boots.*)

2 Ask students these questions as they study and manipulate the TRAP-A-FISH model:

🦃 What did the Wampanoag of long ago use for fishing? (*spears, nets, hooks and lines, traps*)

🦃 Why did the Pilgrims need to learn about fishing from the Wampanoag? (*They needed fish for food, but were not fishermen and knew nothing about the local waters or fish.*)

3 Let students revisit the Pilgrim town and Wampanoag village (see page 17) and take note of the fish-smoking racks, the canoe, and the hunters and fishermen there.

Pilgrim Diary

Invite students to write an entry about having just returned from an imaginary hunting trip with the Wampanoag. What was it like in the woods? What animals did they see? What advice did the Wampanoag share with them? What did they catch? Encourage students to illustrate their entries.

Clam Curiosity

Let students find out more about clams and mussels. What group of animals do they belong to? Are they fish? How do they eat and live? Can they move?

Hunt for Food Match-Up

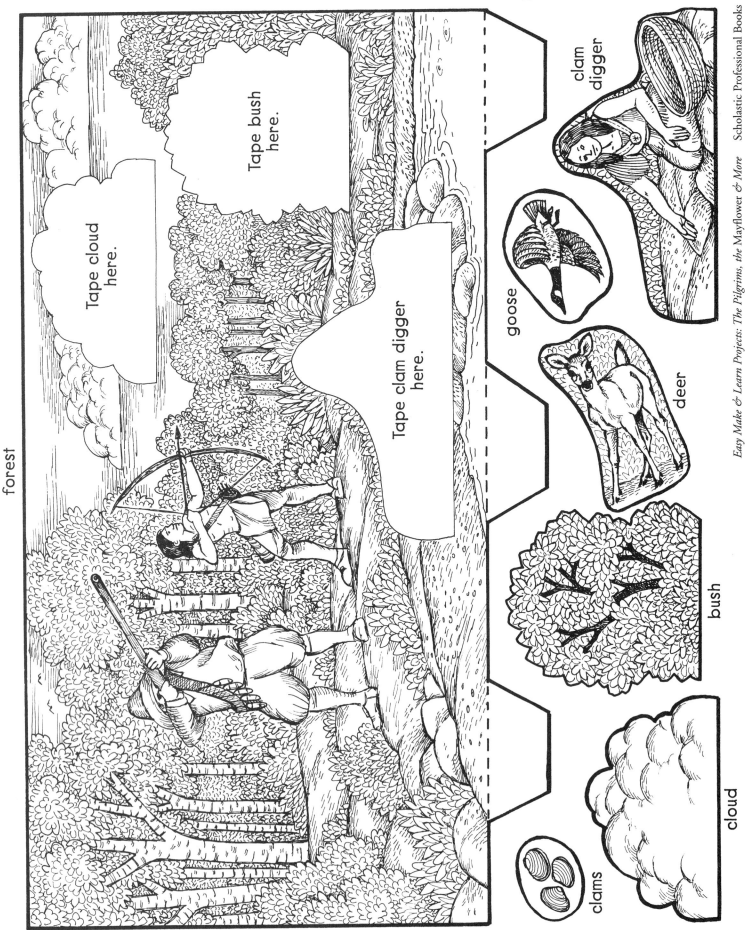

forest

Tape cloud here.

Tape bush here.

Tape clam digger here.

clam digger

goose

deer

bush

clams

cloud

Easy Make & Learn Projects: The Pilgrims, the Mayflower & More   Scholastic Professional Books

✳ Trap a Fish ✳

Easy Make & Learn Projects: The Pilgrims, the Mayflower & More   Scholastic Professional Books

fish

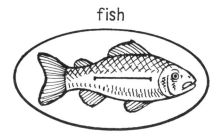

slider

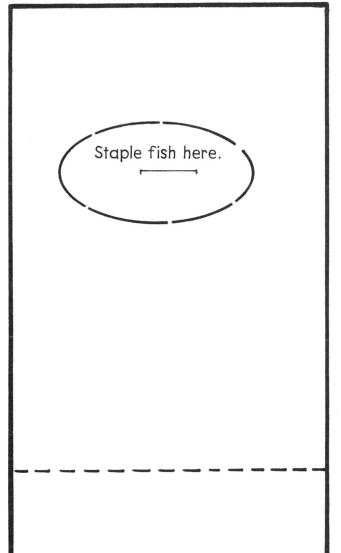

Staple fish here.

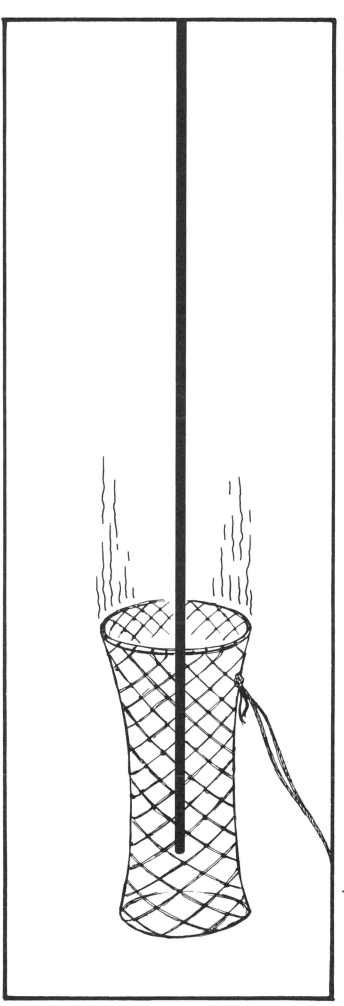

net

What's Cooking? Double Diorama

*With this model, students can get a close-up look
at how foods were prepared by the Pilgrims
and the Wampanoag of long ago.*

❊ A Look Back in Time ❊

Inside each Pilgrim house was a fireplace for warmth and cooking. Copper kettles for boiling lobsters and other foods hung over open flames, meats roasted on spits, and fish sizzled on iron grills. The Pilgrims shared a common outdoor oven for baking bread and pies made with flour ground from grain by the women and children. They stored food in sacks and barrels kept in the lofts and cool, dark cellars of their one-room houses. They also hung fruits, vegetables, and herbs to dry so that the foods would last, especially during the cold winter months.

The Wampanoag of the seventeenth century did most of their cooking outdoors. Outside the round houses, or wetus, the Wampanoag made a roasting spit of two forked sticks on either side of a fire, with a third stick balanced between the two forks. Meat and fish hanging from the stick were roasted, smoked, or dried over the fire. The corn and other vegetables the Wampanoag grew formed the main part of their diets. They boiled ground cornmeal in clay pots and prepared acorn mash. The Wampanoag taught the Pilgrims how to cook corn and vegetable stews such as succotash.

Making the Model

1 Photocopy pages 47 and 48. Color, if desired. Cut out the six pieces along the solid black lines.

2 Cut along the solid black line on the large cooking scene. Then fold the scene along the dotted lines to form a T shape, as shown.

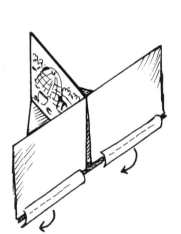

3 Set the T-shaped piece on the dotted line on the triangle pattern. Tape it into place.

4 Fold back the flaps on the stand-up figures, and tape them in front of their respective cooking scenes. Also tape each text label to the front of the appropriate scene.

MATERIALS

- reproducible pages 47–48
- scissors
- tape
- crayons, colored pencils, or markers (optional)

Explore More!

Make a Wampanoag Recipe

The Wampanoag called this corn pudding *nausamp* (nuh-SAMP). Make it with your class to let students sample a food commonly eaten by the Wampanoag.

- **Hominy Grits (preferably coarse)**
- **1/2 cup finely chopped parsley**
- **1/2 cup finely chopped scallions**

Cook the hominy following the directions on the package, adding only salt. Then stir in the chopped parsley and scallions. Add a little boiling water if the mixture is too thick.

Recipe from *Giving Thanks* by Kate Waters (Scholastic, 2001). Used by permission of the author.

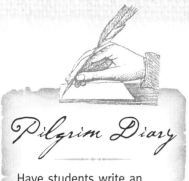

Pilgrim Diary

Have students write an entry describing and drawing what they ate for breakfast, lunch, and supper as Pilgrims. If possible, share passages from *Eating the Plates* by Lucille Recht Penner (see Resources, page 72) for a fascinating and detailed look at the Pilgrims' eating habits. The book also includes authentic Pilgrim recipes.

Teaching With the Model

1 After students have assembled their models, ask them to compare how the Pilgrims and the Wampanoag of long ago cooked. Ask students where the Pilgrims cooked. (*inside the house, in the fireplace*) The Wampanoag? (*outside, over fires*)

2 Give each student a photocopy of page 49. Challenge students to look at each food listed on their WHAT'S COOKING? chart and try to find the food on the model. Tell students to put a check in the appropriate column on their chart. Then ask:

🐚 Did the Pilgrims and the Wampanoag eat the same foods? (*some, but not all*)

🐚 Name a food that the Wampanoag prepared or ate that the Pilgrims did not. (*acorn mash, succotash, sumac tea*) Name a food that the Pilgrims prepared or ate but the Wampanoag didn't. (*corn bread, pies, cheese*)

🐚 Why do you think these different people ate many of the same foods? (*both had to eat what was available*)

🐚 Why did the Pilgrims and Wampanoag dry foods? (*They dried foods such as fish, herbs, and vegetables to preserve them so that they would have enough to eat in winter.*)

3 Invite students to revisit the Pilgrim town and Wampanoag village (see page 17) and take note of the fish-smoking racks, the outdoor village oven, gardens, and who is cooking.

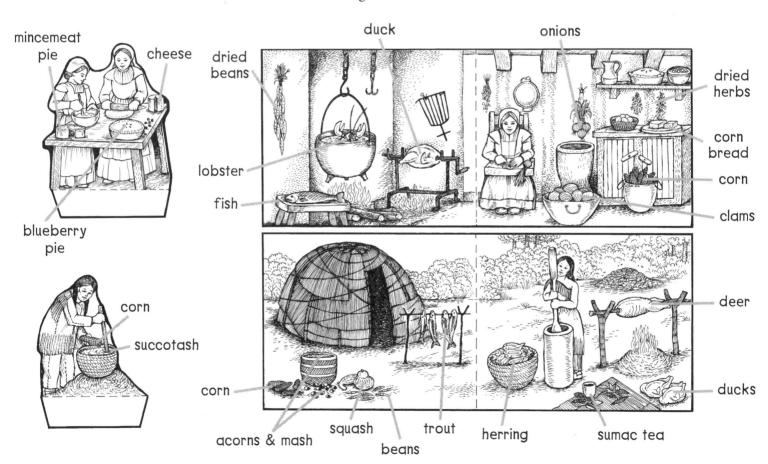

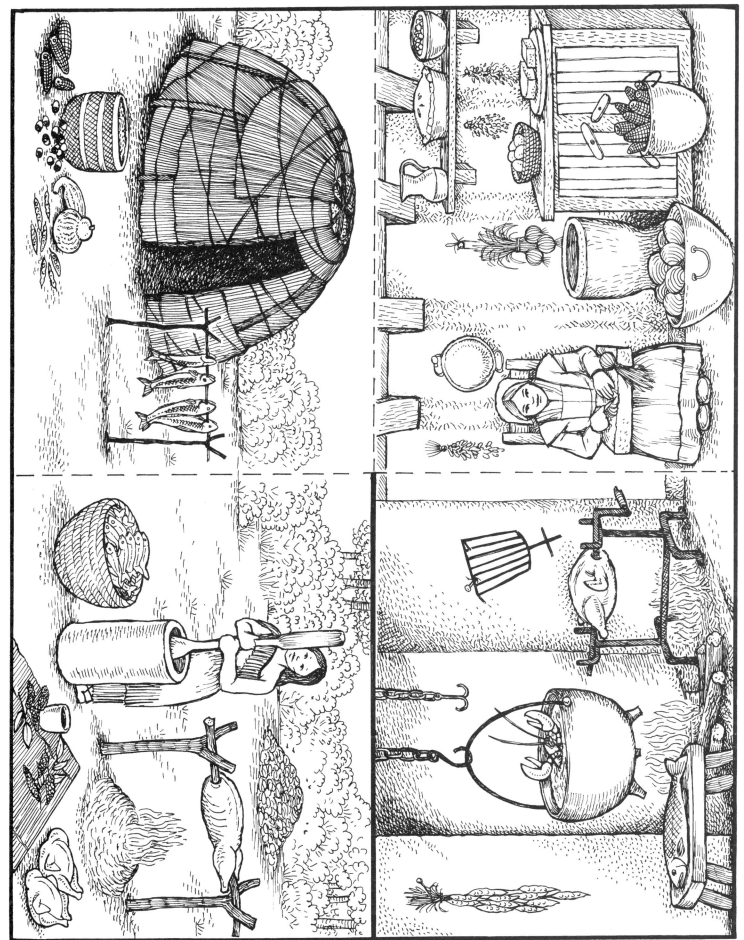

What's Cooking?
Double Diorama

What foods are these Pilgrims preparing?

What foods are these Wampanoag preparing?

Easy Make & Learn Projects: The Pilgrims, the Mayflower & more   Scholastic Professional Books

What's Cooking?

Look for each of the foods listed below on your model. Make a ✔ for each one you find.

	Pilgrims	Wampanoag
duck		
succotash		
onions		
acorns and mash		
corn		
cheese		
sumac tea		
dried herbs		
dried beans		

	Pilgrims	Wampanoag
deer		
clams		
herring and dried fish		
corn bread		
beans		
squash		
blueberry and mincemeat pies		
fish and lobster		

Easy Make & Learn Projects: The Pilgrims, the Mayflower & More   Scholastic Professional Books

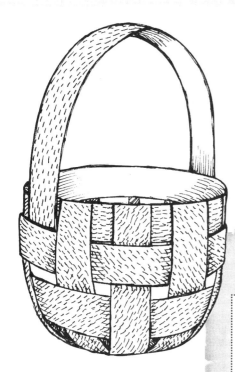

Wampanoag Basket-by-Numbers

Children make a basket and learn about Wampanoag basket making.

❈ A Look Back in Time ❈

Basket making is an ancient handicraft originally employed in the making of storage containers. Techniques for weaving baskets were handed down through generations of Wampanoag and continue to be used today. The Wampanoag traded their baskets with the Pilgrims in exchange for cloth and metal tools. Both groups used baskets for carrying food and other valuable items. The Wampanoag also used them during prayer ceremonies, weddings, and burials and attached spiritual significance to them.

Plants used for basket making had to be collected, cut, split, smoothed, and often beaten until flexible enough to be molded by hand without breaking. Some baskets were woven over and under like cloth, using flexible grasses. Others were coiled and sewn. Still others had a bottom and sides made of rigid sticks.

Making the Model

1 Photocopy page 53. Cut out the eight strips along the solid black lines. Color the strips on both sides, if desired.

2 Wrap the multi-numbered strip into a loop and tape the ends where indicated.

MATERIALS

- reproducible page 53
- scissors
- tape
- crayons, colored pencils, or markers (optional)

3 Tape the short strip number 1 to a 1 on the loop, as shown.

4 Tape the strip's other end to the other 1 on the loop.

5 Repeat steps 3 and 4 with numbered strips 2, 3, and 4.

6 Weave the TOP strip over and under the taped strips, as shown. Tape the overlapping ends together.

7 Repeat step 6 with the BOTTOM strip, weaving it under where the TOP strip went over and over where the TOP strip went under.

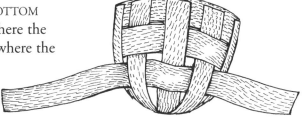

8 Tape the handle strip onto the top loop on opposite sides of the basket.

Pilgrim Diary

Ask students to use imagination to write an entry reporting on the day's trading activities with the Wampanoag. Invite them to draw a picture of the basket or baskets they traded for and the objects they offered in exchange.

Basket Discovery

Bring in different kinds of baskets and invite students to do the same. Challenge students to examine the baskets to determine whether they were woven, coiled, sewn, or made with a combination of methods, and to notice the different patterns that were used.

Teaching With the Model

1 After students have assembled their baskets, ask:

- How did the Pilgrims and Wampanoag of long ago both use baskets? (*for carrying and storing things*)
- How else did the Wampanoag use baskets? (*for spiritual ceremonies*)
- What were Wampanoag baskets made of? (*reeds and other grasses that had been cut, split, smoothed, and beaten until flexible, and sticks*)

2 Invite students to revisit the Pilgrim town and Wampanoag village (see page 17) and look for the baskets used in each.

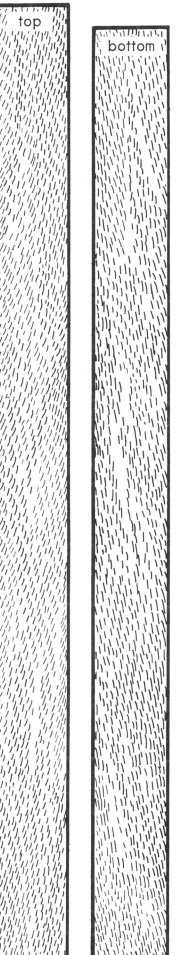

Tape here.

1

2

3

4

1

2

3

4

handle

top

bottom

Wampanoag Basket-by-Numbers

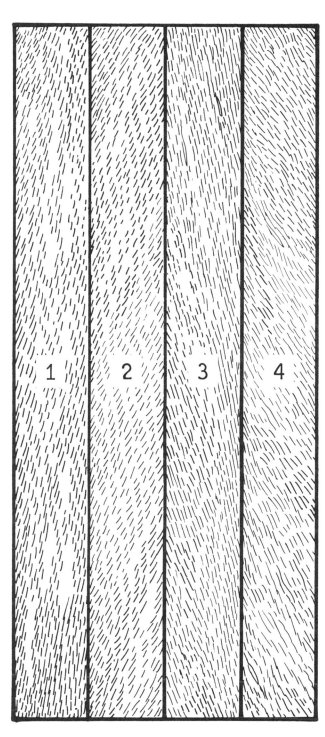

1   2   3   4

Who Wore What? Wardrobes

✳ ✳ ✳

Make & Wear Wampanoag Pouch

Children make models that show how the Pilgrims and Wampanoag of long ago dressed. Then they make a Wampanoag pouch to wear themselves.

✳ A Look Back in Time ✳

The Pilgrims brought clothes with them from Europe and replaced them with homemade clothes as needed. Pilgrim men wore knee-length pants called britches; a large, loose-fitting shirt; a waistcoat (doublet); stockings; garters to hold up the stockings; and shoes or boots. For special occasions they put on ruffled collars and cuffs on top of their waistcoats. Pilgrim women wore a shirtlike shift and petticoats under a gown or under a jacket and a skirt. Their shoes, stockings, and garters were like the men's. Often women wore aprons and covered their heads with a linen bonnet. When outside, the Pilgrims wore capes, loose-fitting outer coats, and felt hats.

Both boys and girls wore dresses until they were seven years old. After that the boys dressed like their fathers and girls like their mothers.

Compared to the Pilgrims, the Wampanoag of long ago wore few clothes. Men and boys wore an animal skin loincloth around their waists. Women and girls wore deerskin dresses. In winter all members of the family would put on leggings, moccasins, and fur pelts from bears, beavers, and other animals to stay warm.

The Wampanoag often wore a deerskin pouch around their neck or tied to their waist belt. In it they carried dried corn to eat while hunting or on a journey. They sometimes decorated the pouches with wampum designs.

Making the Models

Who Wore What? Wardrobes

MATERIALS

- reproducible pages 58–61
- scissors
- tape
- crayons, colored pencils, or markers (optional)

1 Photocopy pages 58 and 59. (Enlarge, if possible.) Color, if desired. Cut out all ten pieces on the two pages along the solid black lines. Then assemble the model as follows:

- Place the STOCKINGS, GARTERS, AND SHOES piece over the PILGRIM FAMILY piece. Tape it as a flap where indicated, on the left side only.

- Place the BRITCHES AND SKIRTS piece on the model and tape it as a flap where indicated, on the left side only. Make sure both flaps open freely.

- Place the APRONS AND WAISTCOATS piece on the model and tape it as a flap where indicated, on the left side only.

- Tape the BONNETS and HATS to their appropriate owners and the basket of corn to the grasp of either the girl or woman.

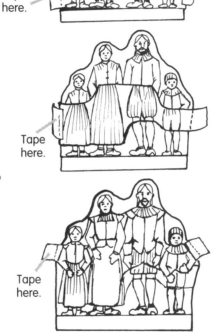

2 Photocopy pages 60 and 61. Color, if desired. Cut out all nine pieces on the two pages along the solid black lines. Then assemble the model as follows:

- Place the LEGGINGS AND MOCCASINS piece over the WAMPANOAG FAMILY piece. Tape it as a flap where indicated, on the right side only.

- Place the FUR PELTS piece on the model and tape it as a flap where indicated, on the right side only.

- Tape the BASKET to the grasp of either the girl or the woman. Tape the POUCHES around the necks of their appropriate owners, as shown. (The basket and pouches can go under or over the fur pelts.)

3 Attach a stand to each model. First, fold a stand piece along the dotted line and tape it to the back of a model, as shown. Then, fold the bottom of the model back to complete the stand, as shown.

Make & Wear Wampanoag Pouch

1 Photocopy page 62. Color, if desired. Cut out the pouch in one piece along the outer solid black lines.

2 Punch two holes at the top, using a hole punch or sharpened pencil.

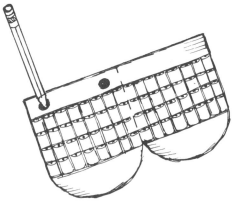

3 Fold the piece along the dotted midline and tape the bottom thoroughly, as shown.

4 Thread one end of the string through a hole and tie a knot in the end so it doesn't slip back through the hole. Repeat for the other hole. Wear the pouch around the neck.

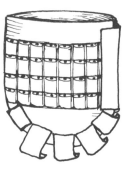

MATERIALS

- reproducible page 62
- scissors
- tape
- sharpened pencil or hole punch
- 2- to 3-foot length of thick string, yarn, or twine
- crayons, colored pencils, or markers (optional)

Teaching With the Models

1 After students have assembled the Pilgrim model, ask:

🕊 How do Pilgrim clothes compare to what people wear today? (*more conservative, less comfortable, and so on*)

🕊 Where did they get their clothes? (*brought some with them, then made them*)

🕊 Did men and women wear different clothes? (*yes*)

2 After students have assembled the Wampanoag model, ask:

🕊 Where did they get their clothes? (*made them from animal skins*)

🕊 Did men and women wear different clothes? (*yes*)

🕊 What do you think modern-day Wampanoag wear? (*mostly modern-day clothing but some may wear traditional garments for religious ceremonies, harvest celebrations, and other special occasions*)

3 Invite students to compare the Wampanoag and Pilgrim clothing:

🕊 Which do you think was easier to make?

🕊 Which do you think was more comfortable?

4 Bring in some unpopped popcorn, and invite students to carry it in their pouches as the Wampanoag did with dried corn. Ask students: What do you think the Wampanoag carried in the pouches? (*food for a journey*)

5 Invite students to revisit the Pilgrim town and Wampanoag village (see page 17) and take note of what the residents are wearing in each.

Pilgrim Diary

Have each student write an entry, as a Pilgrim, that describes getting dressed in the morning. Students can also draw pictures of what they wear.

Explore More!

Make Natural Dyes

It's a popular notion that the Pilgrims wore only dark, somber colors such as brown and black. In fact, red, blue, yellow, violet, and green are also among the colors they wore. The Pilgrims used flowers, leaves, roots, bark, nutshells, and berries to dye the yarn or fabric they made into clothing. Let children experiment with using some of these materials to dye fabric. Fill a reclosable plastic sandwich bag with about 1/4 cup of warm water. Add about 2 tablespoons of plant parts (such as crushed onion skins, grated beets or red cabbage, or spinach leaves). Tell students to squish the plant matter inside the bag for a few minutes and observe the changes. Experiment using these liquid dyes to color cotton cloth.

Who Wore What?
Wardrobes

Easy Make & Learn Projects: The Pilgrims, the Mayflower & More   Scholastic Professional Books

family in shirts

Pilgrim family

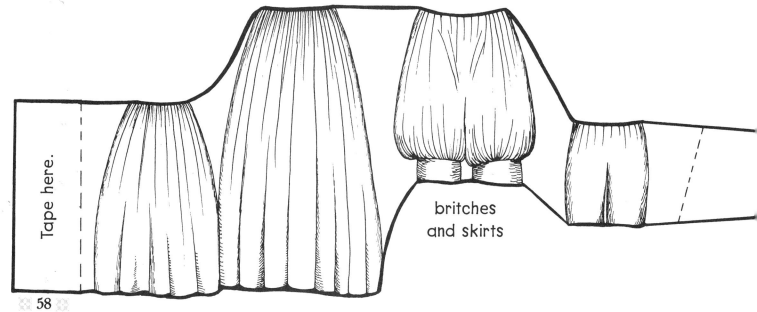

Tape here.

britches and skirts

58

Who Wore What?
Wardrobes

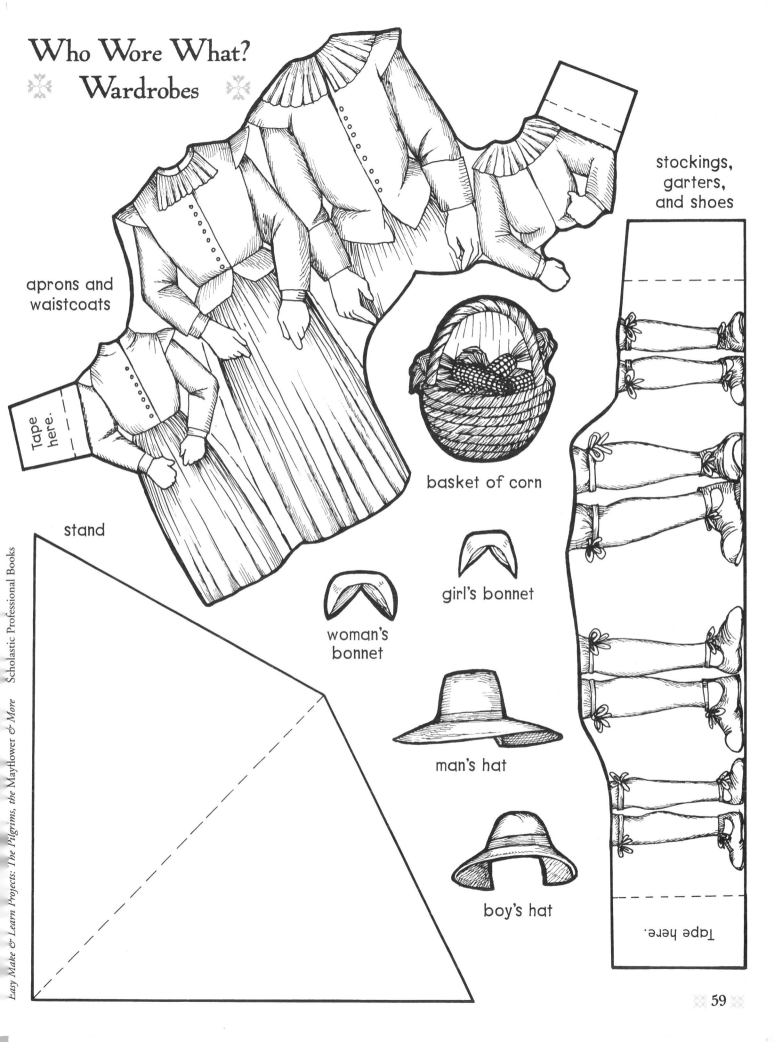

aprons and
waistcoats

stockings,
garters,
and shoes

Tape here.

stand

basket of corn

woman's
bonnet

girl's bonnet

man's hat

boy's hat

Tape here.

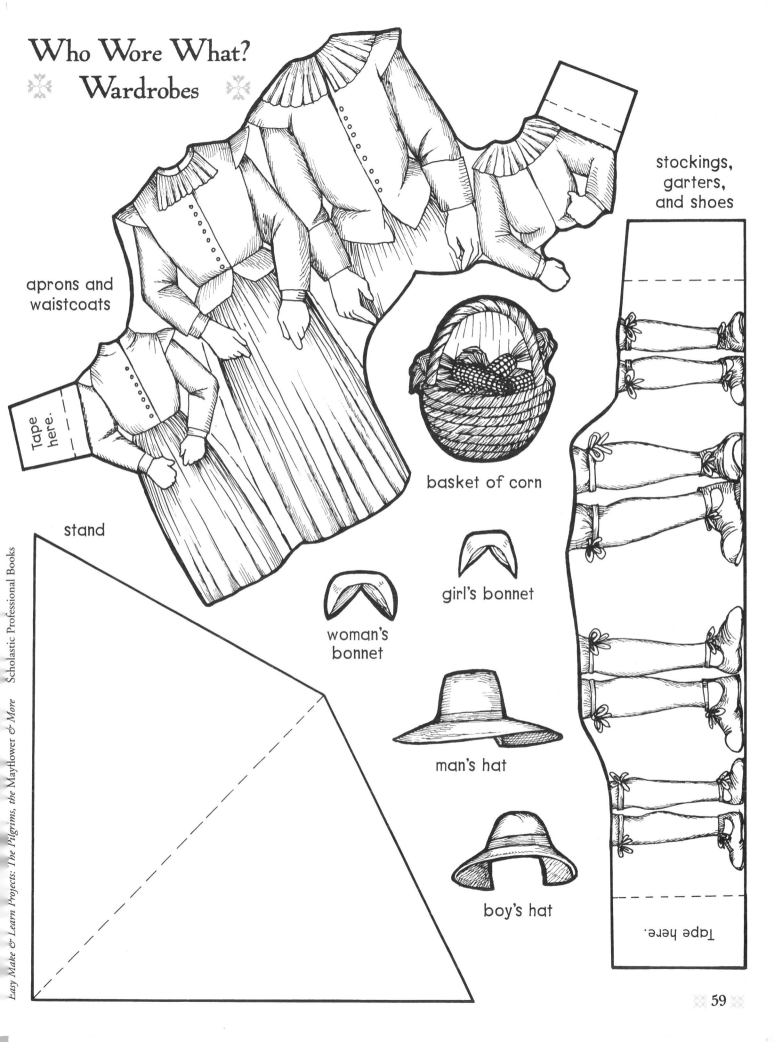

Easy Make & Learn Projects: The Pilgrims, the Mayflower & More   Scholastic Professional Books

Who Wore What?
❊ Wardrobes ❊

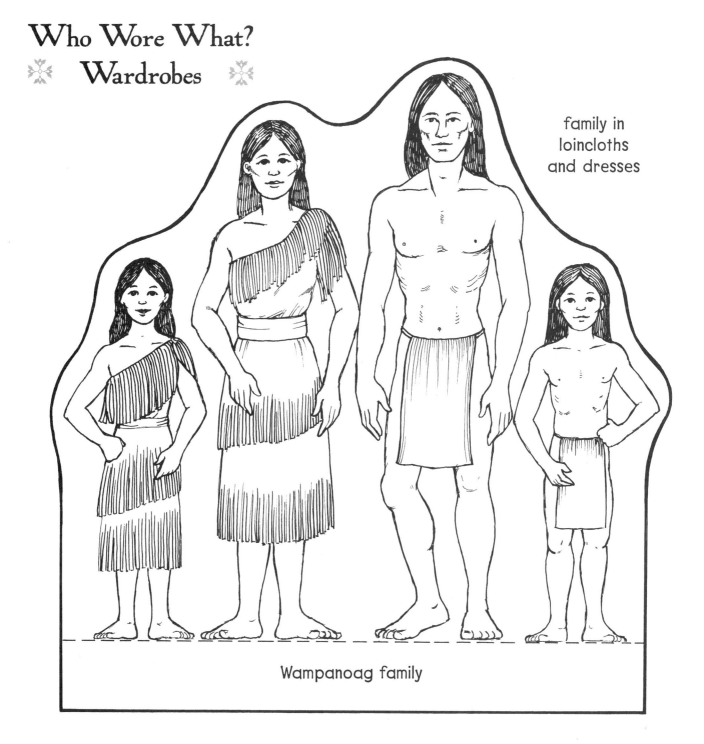

family in
loincloths
and dresses

Wampanoag family

girl's pouch

woman's pouch

man's pouch

boy's pouch

Easy Make & Learn Projects: The Pilgrims, the Mayflower & More Scholastic Professional Books

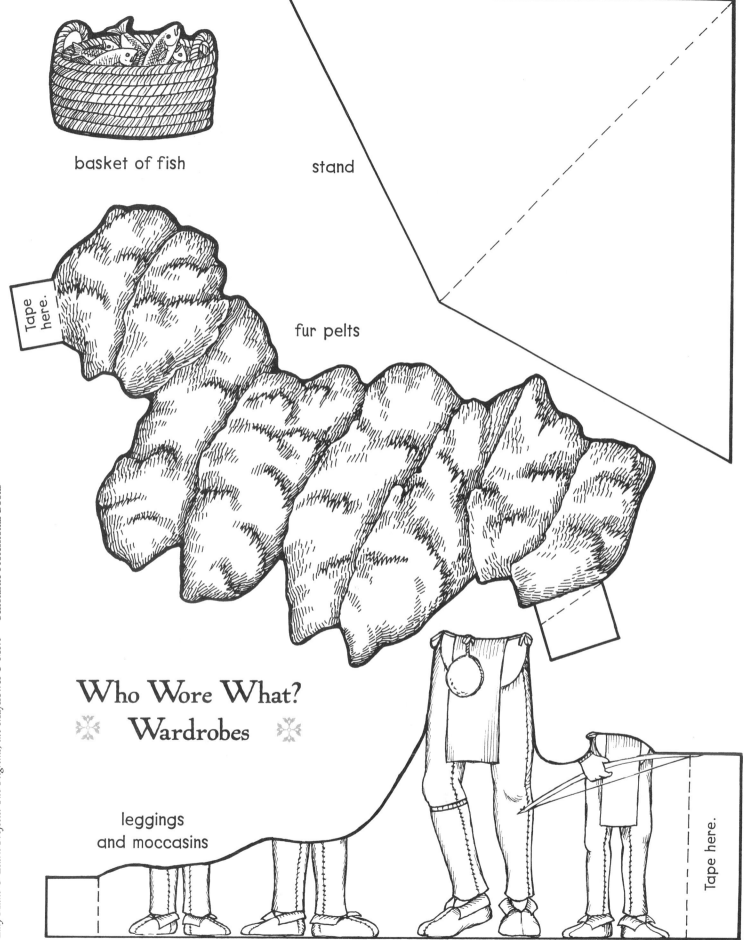

basket of fish

stand

fur pelts

Tape here.

Who Wore What?
❄ Wardrobes ❄

leggings and moccasins

Tape here.

Easy Make & Learn Projects: The Pilgrims, the Mayflower & More · Scholastic Professional Books

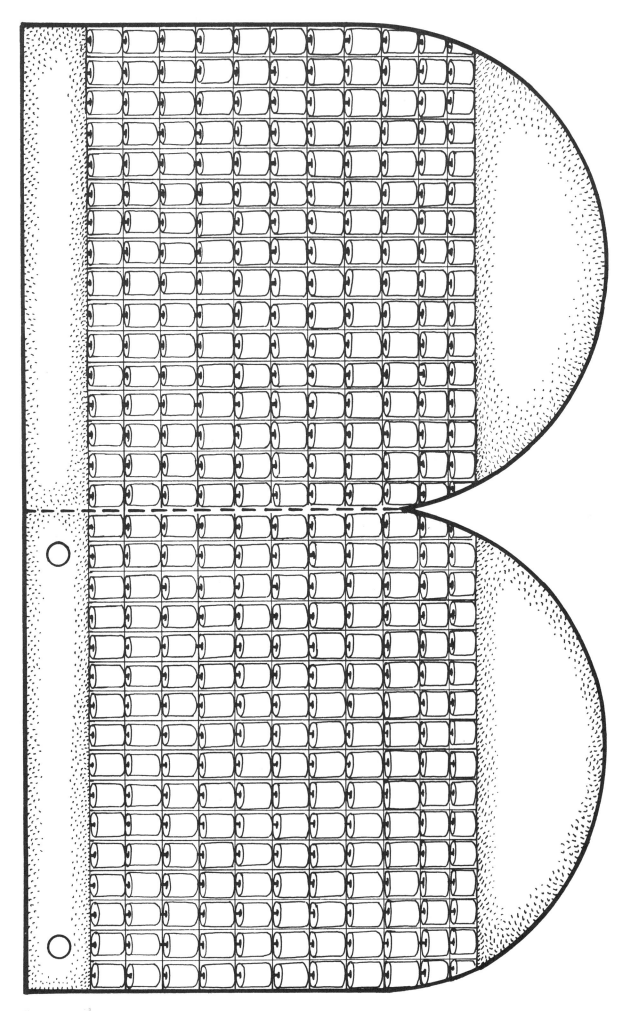

Easy Make & Learn Projects: The Pilgrims, the Mayflower & More   Scholastic Professional Books

Make & Wear Wampum

Children make belts, bracelets, and armbands that simulate the wampum used by the Wampanoag of long ago.

❋ A Look Back in Time ❋

Wampum possesses a rich spiritual and historical meaning in Native American culture. Wampum was made up of purple and white beads created from the hard, rounded shells of quahog clams. The shells were carved into tube-shaped beads about an eighth of an inch in diameter and about a quarter inch long. Tiny holes were drilled into each bead, and then they were strung together or sewn onto fabrics or animal skins. The beads were used to make belts and ceremonial jewelry. Native Americans who lived long ago often wove thousands of beads into wampum belts that were exchanged as pledges to keep treaties and to assure friendships. They also recorded events on their belts by arranging beads in various designs.

When European explorers started trading with East Coast Native Americans, they exchanged cloth and other goods for wampum. The explorers then traded the wampum for furs from other Native Americans. This is how wampum developed into a kind of currency.

Making the Model

1. Photocopy page 65. Cut out all 11 pieces along the solid black lines.

2. Color the quahog clamshell gray on its outside, then turn it over and color its inside purple, leaving some areas white. (The amount of purple varies from shell to shell.)

3. Color the CIRCLE SHELL piece with designs "carved" on it, fold it along the dotted line, and tape as shown.

MATERIALS

- reproducible page 65
- scissors
- tape
- string
- purple and gray crayons, colored pencils, or markers

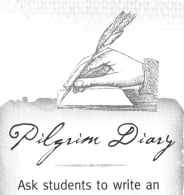

Pilgrim Diary

Ask students to write an entry about seeing their first wampum belt. Have them draw it and then write what it's made of and what the Wampanoag told them the design means.

Explore More!

Beads Tell a Story

Invite students to make a beaded pendant that tells a story, describes an event, or recalls a special memory. Provide beads in different colors (or dyed pasta), glue, and cardboard shapes (circles, triangles, and so on). Encourage students to create designs and patterns with the beads. When they are satisfied with their design, students can glue the beads to the cardboard. When dry, punch a hole in the cardboard and string with yarn to wear.

4 Decorate, color, and tape the other two CIRCLE SHELL pieces.

5 The seven rectangular grid pieces represent wampum beads, 40 per grid. On the one with a design, color the shaded grid squares purple and leave the others white.

6 Create designs for the other rectangles of beads by coloring some of the grid squares purple and leaving others white.

7 Fashion the beads and circles into belts, armbands, necklaces, or bracelets, as shown in the finished model picture. Here are some ideas:

❋ Tape the rectangular pieces end to end to make armbands or headbands.

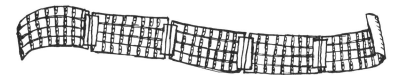

❋ Tape the rectangular pieces onto a double strand of string to make a belt.

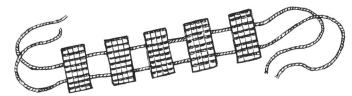

❋ Wrap the rectangular pieces into loops, and close with tape. These cylindrical pieces can be strung into belts or necklaces. You can string the circle pieces along with them, as shown.

Teaching With the Model

1 As students color and create their wearable wampum, discuss what wampum was and what it meant to Native Americans and European explorers.

🐚 What was wampum made of? (*beads carved from quahog clamshells*)

🐚 What was made out of wampum beads? (*belts and ceremonial jewelry*)

🐚 How was wampum used by explorers? (*as currency for furs*)

2 Invite students to revisit the Wampanoag village (see page 17) and find the pile of clamshells near the waste pile. What were all these shells used for?

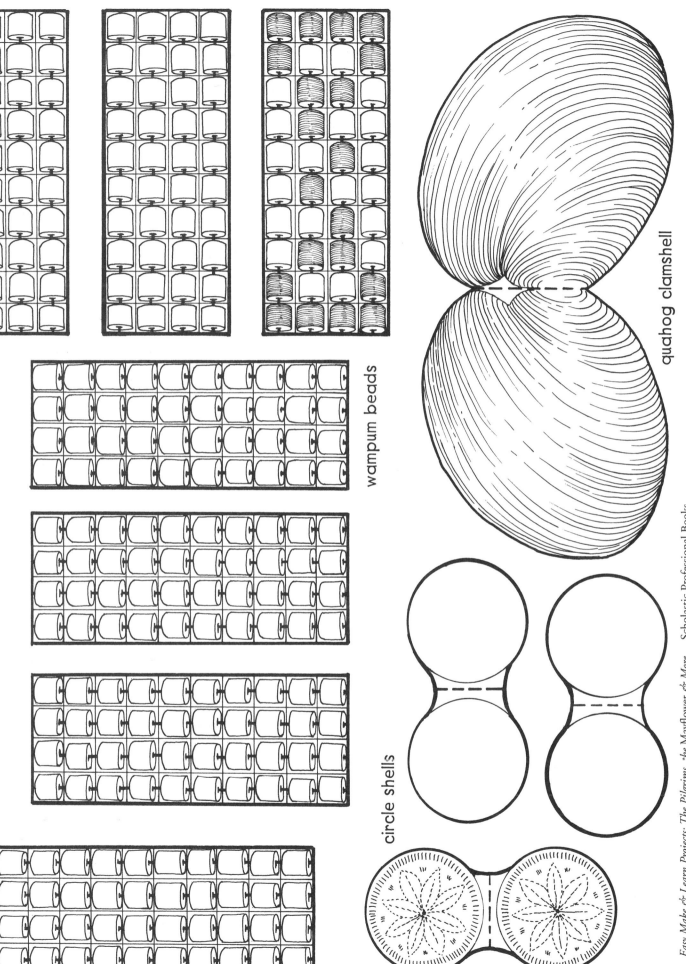

Make & Wear Wampum

wampum beads

quahog clamshell

circle shells

Easy Make & Learn Projects: The Pilgrims, the Mayflower & More   Scholastic Professional Books

Harvest Feast Fun-Fact Scroll

Children make an interactive scroll that lets them discover the traditions behind Thanksgiving.

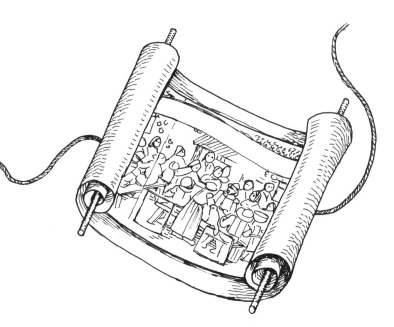

❋ A Look Back in Time ❋

By the spring of 1621 many Pilgrims had died of disease and other causes. When autumn came the Pilgrims harvested acres of corn, barley, peas, and other crops. Then the Pilgrims declared a three-day feast. At this time, Massasoit, the sachem (chief or leader) of a Wampanoag village located some distance away (in what is now known as Bristol, Rhode Island), chose to visit the Pilgrims' village. With his wife and 90 Wampanoag braves, Massasoit made the two-day journey by foot. When the Wampanoag arrived, they joined the surviving 51 Pilgrims in their festivities. For the feast the Pilgrims hunted geese, ducks, and turkeys and caught fish. For their part, the Wampanoag brought five deer. At the feast the Pilgrims marched, the Wampanoag shot arrows at targets, and children played. The Pilgrims were thankful for their health, homes, harvest, and the help they'd received from the Wampanoag.

The custom of Thanksgiving Day spread from Plymouth to other parts of New England and was later celebrated as a holiday in many states. The first president to proclaim Thanksgiving a holiday was Lincoln, who set aside the last Thursday in November 1863 as "…a day of thanksgiving and praise to our beneficent Father." Today at Thanksgiving people still give thanks for all they have, and many also remember the Pilgrims and the Native Americans who helped them.

The Wampanoag celebrated many "Thanksgivings" long before the arrival of the Pilgrims in 1620. At these seasonal harvest festivals, still celebrated throughout the year, the Wampanoag express their gratitude for the gifts of the land. In July, for example, they celebrate a Green Corn Thanksgiving. (Green corn is immature, but edible and sweet.) In October they have a Cranberry Thanksgiving.

Making the Model

1 Reproduce pages 69 and 70. Color, if desired. Cut out the nine pieces along the solid black lines.

2 Place the pages horizontally, and tape or glue the left edge of page 69 to the right edge of page 70 where indicated.

3 Cut the three slits along the solid black lines.

MATERIALS

- reproducible pages 69 and 70
- scissors
- tape
- crayons, colored pencils, or markers (optional)
- 2 thin sticks or dowels, each about 12 inches long
- 12-inch piece of string or ribbon

4 Insert the animals in the appropriate slits and tape into place from the back, as shown.

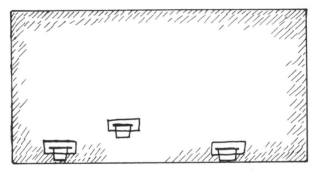

5 Place each of the four squares over the text boxes in the HARVEST FEAST piece so that the squares blend into the scene. Tape the squares at the top to create lift-and-look flaps, as shown.

6 Tape each stick onto one end of the scroll. Then roll up the scroll from both ends and tie in the middle with string or ribbon.

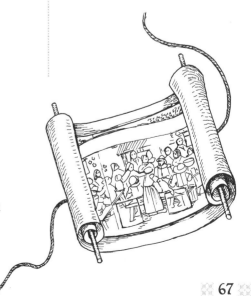

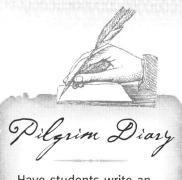

Pilgrim Diary

Have students write an entry about attending the three-day feast. What preparations were made? What did the Wampanoag bring? What did they eat? What did they do for fun? Encourage them to draw pictures of the food, the Pilgrims, and the Wampanoag.

Classroom Celebration

Near Thanksgiving, invite students to reenact the Pilgrims' harvest feast. To make the celebration realistic, challenge them to draw on what they've learned about how the Wampanoag and Pilgrims dressed and ate.

Teaching With the Model

1 Assess what students know about Thanksgiving by asking:

🦃 When is Thanksgiving celebrated? (*autumn, November*)
🦃 Why do we celebrate Thanksgiving? (*to give thanks for what we have; to remember the Pilgrims and helpful Wampanoag people*)
🦃 What can you share about your family's Thanksgiving traditions?

2 After students have assembled their models and lifted the flaps to find the answers to the questions, discuss the connection between Thanksgiving and the Pilgrims' first harvest celebration.

🦃 Why did the Pilgrims declare a harvest feast? (*to eat, celebrate, rest, and play*)
🦃 For what were the Pilgrims thankful? (*the harvest, their homes, their survival, the help they received from the Wampanoag*)
🦃 Who shared the feast with the Pilgrims? (*Massasoit, his wife, and 90 Wampanoag braves*)
🦃 How had the Wampanoag helped the Pilgrims? (*They taught the Pilgrims how to plant corn, hunt, and fish.*)

3 Invite students to revisit the Pilgrim town (see page 17) and find the large table near the meetinghouse where part of the harvest celebration may have taken place. Students can move the traveling braves from the Wampanoag village to the Pilgrim town, near the table.

vest Feast 1621

Were there more Pilgrims or Wampanoag at the feast?

The Wampanoag brought five deer.

What did the Wampanoag bring?

There were more Wampanoag than Pilgrims at the feast.

What did the diners use to eat their food?

Food was eaten with hands, knives, and spoons.

Easy Make & Learn Projects: The Pilgrims, the Mayflower & More Scholastic Professional Books

Tape or glue to left edge of page 69.

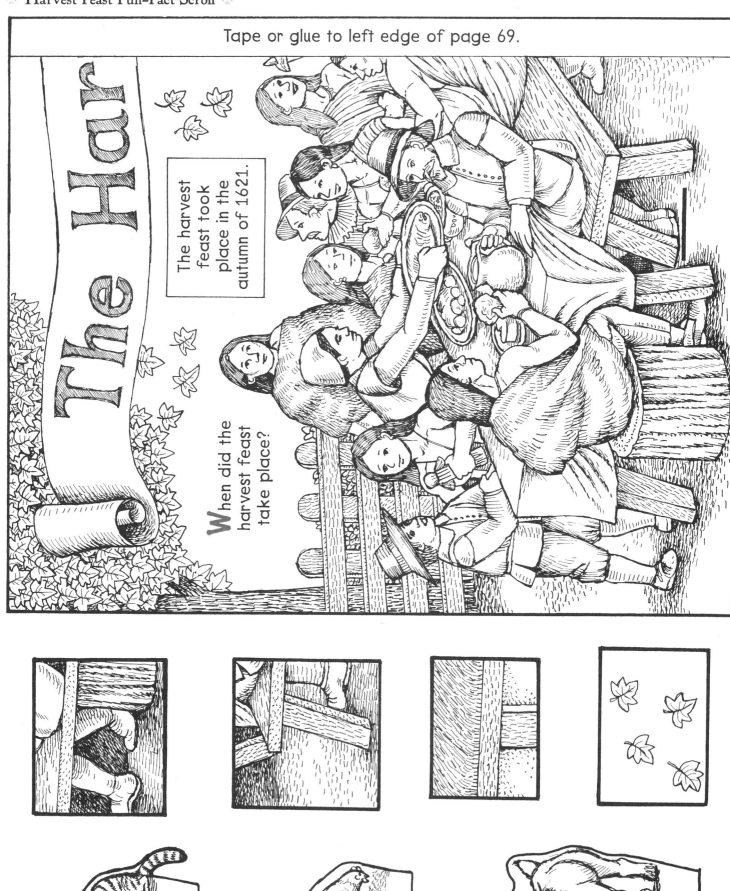

The Har

The harvest feast took place in the autumn of 1621.

When did the harvest feast take place?

❄ Resources ❄

Books for Teachers

The First Peoples of the Northeast by Esther K. Braun (Moccasin Hill Press, 1994). This resource provides a thorough look at Native American life in the northeast.

Fresh & Fun: Thanksgiving by Kathleen M. Hollenbeck (Scholastic, 1999). This fun resource is chock-full of cross-curricular activities relating to the origin and meaning of Thanksgiving.

The Pequots in Southern New England edited by Laurence M. Hauptman and James D. Wherry (University of Oklahoma Press, 1993). The information in this excellent book about the Pequot Indians and how they lived also applies to other Algonquian tribes, including the Wampanoag.

Pilgrims: Complete Theme Unit Developed in Cooperation With the Pilgrim Hall Museum by Susan Moger (Scholastic, l995). Not only does this wonderful book relate the story of the Pilgrims but it also includes cross-curricular activities along with a poster of the *Mayflower*.

Plimoth Plantation: A Pictoral Guide by James W. Baker (Plimoth Plantation Inc., 1997). This comprehensive story and guidebook to the Pilgrims at Plimoth Plantation is full of interesting information not found in other resources.

The Thanksgiving Activity Book by Deborah Schecter (Scholastic, 2000). The creative and fun activities in this book will help students make a personal connection with this harvest holiday. Includes a *Mayflower* board game, a Thanksgiving Memories mini-book, riddles, art activities, poems, songs, a pocket-chart poetry poster, and more.

Wampanoag: People of the East (Plimoth Plantation Educational Materials). This valuable resource, published by Plimoth Plantation, contains detailed information about the history and rich culture of the Wampanoag people.

Web Sites

The Boston Children's Museum
www.bostonkids.org

The Boston Children's Museum site includes information about the history, culture, and heritage of the Wampanoag Indians as well as suggested readings, activities, and examples taken from the museum's Native American collection. A highlight of this site is the "Evaluating Resources" page. It offers teachers and other educators 10 specific guidelines for evaluating literature and other resources for bias-free portrayals of Native Americans and accurate information about their cultures.

Pilgrim Hall Museum
www.pilgrimhall.org

In addition to primary sources about the first Thanksgiving, this site includes fascinating photographs of Pilgrim and Wampanoag artifacts from the museum's collections.

Plimoth Plantation
www.plimoth.org

For an exciting and comprehensive look at Pilgrim life, check out this Web site. It features a museum, library, calendar of events, and museum shop full of recommendations for further reading and learning.

Books for Students

Eating the Plates by Lucille Recht Penner (Macmillan, 1991). This wonderful book offers students a wealth of information about the food preparation, cooking techniques, and home life of the Pilgrims. The book also includes a section of authentic Pilgrim recipes.

The First Thanksgiving by Linda Hayward (Random House, 1990). This book presents an easy-to-read history, from the sailing of the *Mayflower* to the first Thanksgiving.

Giving Thanks: The 1621 Harvest Feast by Kate Waters (Scholastic, 2001). This fascinating photo reenactment tells the real story of the famous harvest feast as seen through the eyes of a Wampanoag and a Pilgrim boy.

Homes in the Wilderness: A Pilgrim's Journal of Plymouth Plantation in 1620 by William Bradford and others, edited by Margaret Wise Brown (Linnet Books, 1988). This book features a classic firsthand account of Pilgrim life in the "New World," retold for young readers.

If You Sailed on the Mayflower by Ann McGovern (Scholastic, 1991). A question-and-answer format tells about life on the *Mayflower* and the Pilgrims' first year in America.

North America in Colonial Times: An Encyclopedia for Students edited by Jacob Ernest Cooke and Milton M. Klein (Charles Scribner's Sons, 1998). This four-volume set includes information about the Pilgrims, Plymouth Colony, Massasoit and the Wampanoag Indians, and Thanksgiving.

On the Mayflower: Voyage of the Ship's Apprentice and a Passenger Girl by Kate Waters (Scholastic, 1996). Text and photographs relate the story of two young Pilgrims as they cross the Atlantic Ocean on the *Mayflower* and become friends.

Pilgrim Voices: Our First Year in the New World edited by Connie and Peter Roop (Walker and Company, 1998). In this book the Pilgrims' own words come alive to describe the trials and tribulations of reaching the "New World" and trying to survive there.

Sarah Morton's Day: A Day in the Life of a Pilgrim Girl by Kate Waters (Scholastic, 1989). This delightful book follows a Pilgrim girl as she does her chores and adjusts to life in America.

The Story of Squanto: First Friend to the Pilgrims by Cathy East Dubowski (Gareth Stevens, 1997). This volume presents the life of Squanto and the role he played in the success of the Plymouth colony.

Tapenum's Day: A Wampanoag Indian Boy in Pilgrim Times by Kate Waters (Scholastic, 1996). This vivid story portrays what life might have been like for a young Wampanoag Indian at the time of the Pilgrims.